BUY & BUILD
The Advertising Posters of the Empire Marketing Board

FRONTISPIECE
Artist: Austin Cooper
Title: Follow the Flag in all your Purchases
Displayed: 1927
Printer: George Falkner, Manchester and London
Size: 20 ins. × 30 ins.
EMB ref: SWB8
PRO ref: CO 956/551

PUBLIC RECORD OFFICE

BUY & BUILD

The Advertising Posters of the Empire Marketing Board

STEPHEN CONSTANTINE

University of Lancaster

LONDON   HER MAJESTY'S STATIONERY OFFICE

ISBN 0 11 440200 0

ACKNOWLEDGEMENTS

I am conscious of how many people have assisted me in the preparation of this volume. While none of them can be held responsible for any errors of fact or interpretation, I readily acknowledge my gratitude to their knowledge and skills. I am indebted to the staff at the University of Lancaster Library, Cambridge University Library, the Bodleian Library and Rhodes House Library in Oxford, the Institute of Commonwealth Studies Library in London, Oxford City Library and Durham City Library. I am grateful to the Head of Special Collections for permission to consult the Neville Chamberlain Papers at Birmingham University Library, and to the Rt. Hon. Julian Amery MP for permission to consult the Leo Amery Papers in his possession. Mrs. D. Tallents and Mrs. M, Pemberton-Pigott made memorable my research at Bodicote Manor, and I record with thanks their hospitality and their kindness in allowing me to consult those papers of Sir Stephen Tallents in their possession. Ms. Rachel Hasted of the Lancashire County Museums Service kindly located material for me in the Museum of Childhood, Judges' Lodgings, Lancaster. Several correspondents answered my inquiries, and I am pleased to express thanks to
Mr. T. Snoddy, Mr. G. Williams, Miss Shirin Spencer, Miss Unity Spencer, Mrs. Nancy Carline, Mr. A. Gardner-Medwin as a trustee at the Stanley Spencer Gallery Cookham, Ms. Sarah Fox-Pitt at the Tate Gallery, Ms. Marie Valsamidi at the Royal Academy of Arts, Ms. Sarah Hyde at the Whitworth Art Gallery Manchester, Mr. A. V. Griffiths of the Department of Prints and Drawings at the British Museum, and especially Ms. Margaret Timmers of the Department of Designs, Prints and Drawings at the Victoria and Albert Museum who located and allowed me to see those designs in the V and A collection which whetted my interest in the EMB posters and who has subsequently patiently answered my questions. Some material in the introduction first appeared in an essay published in *Imperialism and Popular Culture* (1986) and I am grateful to Manchester University Press and to the editor, my colleague Dr. John MacKenzie, for permission to re-use it here. This present book, based largely on official records kept at the Public Record Office, is more than usually dependent on the support of the PRO staff. It owes much to the technical skills of those working in the conservation and photography departments and an enormous amount to Dr. Michael Jubb whose own volume on poster history, *Cocoa and Corsets,* was an inspiration to me and who has worked hard in the preparation of this book. I am, of course, also grateful to HMSO and especially to Mr. Philip Glover for his interest in my original proposal and active support. As usual I am grateful to my wife, Wendy, for more than her skills as typist, secretary and critic. In the dedication I refer to those to whom I owe so much for so many reasons.

CONTENTS

FOR MY MOTHER AND FATHER

Introduction

Controversy was never far away from the Empire Marketing Board. The Board was established as a British government department in May 1926 and abolished in September 1933, and during the few years of its existence, its constitution, its financing, its aims and especially its unusual and innovative operations ensured that it was the subject of frequent political and public comment. While some contemporaries condemned it as a 'futile and wasteful institution', others were loud in their praises. *The Times* regarded the EMB as 'the most fruitful and successful experiment in organizing for Imperial development which has yet been made'.[1] Jan Smuts, the former South African prime minister, considered it 'the one bright spot in recent Empire policy'. Some of the excitement generated by the Board is still apparent in the memoirs of those who worked for it. For Leo Amery, the first chairman, 'it was "Heaven to be alive" during those years'.[2]

Historians have found much of interest and significance in the EMB's work. It has been regarded as symptomatic of an increased official commitment to Empire interests, especially economic, in the decades after the First World War. The Board's work has also been described as an attempt to consolidate imperialist ideals and an imperial world view as part of the popular culture of the British people.[3] In another context, emphasis has been placed on the Board's innovative role in the development of government public relations techniques and information services, as a forerunner of the Ministry of Information in the Second World War and of the later Central Office of Information.[4] Attention has been drawn to its activities as an agency for encouraging and financing scientific research into problems of Empire food production and marketing, and the Board has also been widely credited with stimulating and developing the British documentary film movement.[5] This volume has been designed to provide an account of one other distinctive feature of the EMB's work, its poster campaign.[6]

Advertising posters are intended to have an immediate effect upon contemporary society. But like much so-called ephemeral material, they often deserve careful preservation and subsequent study by later generations. The aesthetic qualities of some designs may alone justify their safe-keeping. The Empire Marketing Board came into operation at a time when the profession of poster artist was already well-established and when substantial efforts were being made to raise the artistic quality of the commercial advertising poster. The Board aspired to secure the best from many of the most distinguished designers of the period, and the high quality of much of the work produced, in a remarkable variety of styles, is one reason for preserving the posters and for reproducing a selection in this volume.

Advertising posters can also be informative about the society which produced and viewed them. This does not mean that the pictures in this volume can be taken at face value as objective portraits of the past, however evocative they may appear to be of the United Kingdom and the British Empire between the wars. Like most advertising posters, many contain images, styles of dress, for example, or the shape of motor cars, ships and aeroplanes, which appear to date them immediately to a precise historical period. But we are deceived if we assume that pictures in advertisements are merely reflections of reality. The EMB and its artists selected, constructed and then presented the images in these posters with a purpose. The designs flashed visual messages, which contemporary viewers were expected to read and which were intended to alter their behaviour. Fortunately, when examining the posters today, we may still intercept the messages. By doing so we may decode the aims and identify the assumptions of the EMB and of the governing class which created it. The Board's attempt to harness aesthetic power for political and ideological purposes enhances the value of the posters as historical records.

The Empire Marketing Board published in its lifetime around 800 different designs, mainly as posters for hoardings or for shop window displays. Until quite recently the only well-known collection was kept in the Victoria and Albert Museum in London. Here there are 58 printed posters and 21 original designs. A smaller collection of about 30 posters may be found in Birmingham Polytechnic Library. Otherwise only scattered items appeared to have survived in a few galleries, until in 1977 the Public Record Office took official delivery of over 700 EMB posters. These had been discovered a few years earlier in the Foreign and Commonwealth Office, overlooked and unrecognised. It is from that treasure trove that the designs reproduced in this volume have been chosen. The Public Record Office also holds the minutes and papers of the Board and its various committees plus a little surviving correspondence. When to this are added other government documents in the Public Record Office, the published reports of the EMB, contemporary press comment, the private papers of Sir Stephen Tallents and further miscellaneous sources, an exceptional opportunity is presented. These records can be used to reveal an attempt to use art for official political purposes. The business of commissioning, designing, printing and displaying the work of poster artists can also be followed in detail. And, to a lesser extent, the impact which the campaign had upon the public at which it was aimed can be assessed.

Origins and Aims of the Empire Marketing Board

It is necessary to describe the context in which the Empire Marketing Board was formed before we can understand the purpose of the posters and interpret their content. Since the late 19th century, many politicians and businessmen in Britain had been expressing their concern about the condition and long-term prospects of the British economy. The country's once supreme position as the leading industrial society, the workshop of the world dominating international trade in manufactured goods, was being challenged, and her still important home agricultural interests were being severely damaged by competition from rapidly developing industrial and agricultural rivals, especially the United States, Germany and later Japan. Moreover, the British economy, peculiarly dependent on export markets, was particularly vulnerable when foreign nations began from the 1870s and especially after the First World War to protect their home markets with tariff barriers while remaining at liberty to export their own products to the still largely free-trading home and colonial markets of Great Britain. The First World War further accelerated Britain's relative economic decline, and the result appeared evident with the onset of the postwar economic depression which pushed unemployment rates in the 1920s almost continuously above ten per cent of the insured labour force. Some observers linked these difficulties to the equally alarming emergence over the same period of the organised Labour movement, its socialist philosophy apparently feeding off the discontent among working people engendered by economic problems and depressed living standards.

In this situation, particularly by the 1920s, many businessmen and many politicians of all persuasions, including some in the Labour Party, looked to the British Empire overseas for salvation. Victory in the First World War had added former imperial possessions of Germany and Turkey to the British Empire as mandated territories in Africa, the Pacific and the Middle East. This increased the Empire to its maximum size, incorporating approximately one quarter of the world's land surface and one quarter of its population, seemingly united as subjects of the Crown. Some commentators believed that the climatic and economic variety of this vast Empire offered British traders compensation for markets being lost elsewhere. Judiciously developed, the Empire might become much more economically self-sufficient, less vulnerable to foreign competition. Here, then, was a route to Britain's long-term economic survival, to her political security in the wider world, to higher standards of living in Britain and perhaps, some hoped, to social harmony, social stability and political quiescence at home.

The problem was, of course, to translate these high aspirations into practice. Imperial enthusiasts were often impatient with mere free enterprise and looked to the state to engineer economic development and closer imperial economic ties. And by the 1920s their lobbying and the troublesome context of the time had persuaded governments to provide some funds for colonial development schemes, for scientific research into problems of Empire production and for assisted passages for migrants wishing to settle in the white dominions. But the imperialists' principal proposal was to couple tariff protection around Britain with imperial preference agreements between Britain and Empire countries which would obstruct foreign imports into Britain and the Empire and increase the flows of intra-imperial commerce. Since first launched by Joseph Chamberlain in 1903, this tariff reform programme had been highly contentious, and the controversy which it generated in the 1920s provided the immediate origin of the Empire Marketing Board.[7]

Tariff reformers after the First World War attempted to persuade the Conservative party to embrace their programme. The Conservatives had after all come close to accepting such a policy before the war, and several leading Conservatives were vocal and energetic supporters, particularly Sir Philip Cunliffe-Lister who was President of the Board of Trade in the Bonar Law and Baldwin governments in the 1920s and Leo Amery who had been a junior minister at the Colonial Office after the war and was to become Secretary of State for the Colonies in 1924 and in addition the first Secretary of State for the Dominions in 1925. The rising tide of unemployment and the simultaneous emergence of Labour as the principal Opposition party increased their sense of urgency. Stanley Baldwin was inevitably subjected to much pressure to adopt tariffs and imperial preferences when he became Prime Minister for the first time in May 1923. The governments of the dominions also for the most part pressed for this policy.

Late in 1923 the tariff reform lobby seemed on the brink of success. The dominions persuaded the British government at the Imperial Economic Conference in the autumn to accept the principle of tariff reform and to introduce imperial preferences on a limited range of dominions' foodstuffs imported into Britain. Baldwin shortly afterwards announced a cautious programme of selected tariff reforms in his manifesto for the general election. However, free trade sentiment in the country remained strong, and the fear of higher food prices ensured that at the election in December 1923 the Conservatives lost their overall majority. While the first Labour government spluttered through its brief existence in 1924, the bruised Baldwin was busy backtracking. In the Conservative manifesto for the next election held in October 1924, he pledged that there would be no large-scale tariff protection.

This relapse was unacceptable to the disgruntled dominions and utterly frustrating for Conservative advocates of imperial preference. Cunliffe-Lister tried to salvage something from the setback, and he proposed a compromise, accepted initially with reluctance by Amery and the dominions, but with some relief by Baldwin and the rest of the Cabinet. Instead of the preferential duties promised to the dominions, a rough cash equivalent of up to £1 million a year of British taxpayers' money would be spent by the British government promoting the sale of Empire foodstuffs in Britain at the expense of foreign suppliers. It was, of course, assumed that such sales would increase the purchasing power of the overseas Empire and as a result would assist British exports of manufactured goods. Some modification of the initial proposal was needed once British farmers got wind of it. Increased imports of some dominions' foodstuffs, such as dairy products and fruit, threatened to be at the expense of British suppliers. The point was made forcefully by the Minister of Agriculture. The Cabinet, ever mindful of Conservative interests in the shires, readily agreed that the money should be spent promoting the sale of home as well as overseas Empire foodstuffs.

Once convinced that this was the only way forward, Amery masterminded the establishment and manning of the government department which was to administer the Empire Marketing Fund.[8] The Empire Marketing Board was a constitutional oddity. Technically, the Board was an advisory committee of the Secretary of State for the Dominions. But as he was *ex officio* chairman and authorised its activities, the Board possessed executive authority. It was supported in its planning and expenditure by a civil service staff totalling about 120 people at its maximum.[9] Moreover, the ferocious combat between Secretary of State and Chancellor of the Exchequer, which each year accompanied the determination of the precise allocation of parliamentary money to be given to the Board, largely reflected the remarkable freedom from normal Treasury control of expenditure which Amery had contrived when the Board was set up. It was a liberty which Amery and his colleagues always enjoyed, which encouraged them in their innovations and which the Treasury and their allies always resented. The membership of the Board, normally totalling about twenty, was also peculiar. It reflected the remarkable consensus between leaders of the major political parties in favour of Empire development by being cross-party. Labour leaders like J.H.Thomas served on the Board when Amery was *ex officio* chairman. Amery remained on the Board when the Labour government succeeded the Conservatives in 1929, and he continued to serve when the National government followed on late in 1931. As Thomas put it: 'there are no politics in this...the Empire Marketing Board is an official non-political body'. The consensus of the day also found it acceptable to make this an imperial as well as British advisory board, so that in addition to the ministers representing the British government there were also representatives from India, Southern Rhodesia, the colonies and protectorates and each of the dominions.[10]

The range of operations in which the EMB engaged was also wide and most unusual for a government department. Its activities encompassed much more than the display of advertising posters. Broadly, its work was divided into three sections, each supervised by a committee of the Board. The Research Committee made grants to institutions in Britain and overseas to investigate problems of animal husbandry, entomology, plant breeding, mycology and other matters which affected Empire food production. The Marketing Committee supervised investigations into particular problems affecting food supply and distribution and also published regular information bulletins to inform trade organisations in Britain about British, overseas Empire and foreign foods currently on the market. The Board was always conscious of the priority need to improve the range, quality and quantity of Empire supplies, and accordingly the larger part of its expenditure, almost £2 million, was spent on these research and marketing services. The Board's third concern was the responsibility of the Publicity Committee, the attempt to influence consumer choice and the flow of commerce not by financial means, tariff barriers, but by propaganda. It was an important part of the enterprise, costing nearly £1¼ million, and inevitably it attracted most public notice.[11]

The EMB was aware of the magnitude of the task which confronted it. During the 19th century the United Kingdom had become the centre of a world and not just an imperial economic system. The volume of British imports drawn from the Empire overseas had increased substantially since before the First World War but still constituted only thirty per cent of the total in 1926. Less than half the grain and dairy products imported into Britain came from the Empire, only a quarter of the meat and fruit.[12] The problem was partly one of consumer ignorance about the country of origin of the food on the market. Amery recalls how difficult it was to persuade shopkeepers and customers that Californian tinned fruit was not an Empire product. The Merchandise Marks Act of 1926 went some way to remedy this deficiency by requiring certain imported goods to be more clearly marked with their place of origin, and the Board itself was to be involved in publicising United Kingdom 'national marks'.[13] But the obstacles were more substantial than ignorance, for, as the Cabinet was informed, 'Forty millions of people had to be induced to change their habits'.[14]

The Board's task was complicated by the lack of expertise in publicity or propaganda work within the government service. It is true that the Post Office had been advertising its services since the 1850s, but few other government departments felt the need to publicise or explain their operations to the general public. The First World War, of course, changed all that, but only for its duration. A state system of publicity and propaganda, ultimately under the control of the Ministry of Information, had employed all the media then available, including printed matter, films and posters, to raise recruits, mobilise resources, maintain morale, woo neutrals and discourage the enemy. There were precedents here which the EMB could follow. The Armistice, however, brought the rapid end of the Ministry. Government advertising activities in 1925 cost a mere £35,000. The armed services maintained press officers and advertised for recruits, a few other government departments were obliged to advertise for tenders or to publish statutory notices, and the Foreign Office engaged modestly in some propaganda work. But in effect official propaganda or even publicity operations were virtually eliminated after the war and the expertise dispersed.[15] As the EMB concluded at its first formal meeting in June 1926, they 'had to explore ground that was at some points still unprospected, and would be working on a scale of which no government, except perhaps in war time, had had experience'.[16]

The Board was, however, conscious of the remarkable range of media available for publicity and persuasion which had been exploited by the private sector since the end of the previous century. Cheap mass circulation newspapers, improved techniques of paper-making and printing, photography, cinema and the wireless were all developments which had attracted and in some cases had been stimulated by an increasingly sophisticated advertising industry. And the poster for display on the public hoarding had been transformed. The invention of lithography in 1798 by Alois Senefelder in Germany had little impact on the advertising poster until the invention of the powered printing press made possible the production of long runs of good quality posters at low cost and high speed. By the end of the 19th century further possibilities for poster designs were realised by improvements in colour lithography and typography and by the development of offset rotary presses as a means of reproducing them. Moreover, by this time a new profession of the commercial poster artist had been called into being in response to the requirements of the advertising agent and his clients. By the 1890s the Beggarstaffs and Dudley Hardy had established new standards of English poster art, and John Hassall, Cecil Aldin, Frank Brangwyn and others were to maintain the level in the following decade. Quality was demanded by such innovative and discerning companies as the Metropolitan District Railway and the Orient-Pacific Line, and the First World War provoked some artists like Alfred Leete and Spencer Pryse into the production of effective propaganda posters. After the war, rising living standards, mass consumerism, further developments in the media and a sophisticated exploitation of the opportunities thereby created made the 1920s 'the golden age of advertising'. Total expenditure on advertising in Britain rose from an estimate £31 million in 1920 to £57 million by 1928.[17]

The Board must also have been aware that some commercial companies had already attempted to combine patriotism with profit. Those businesses like Fry's, Cadbury's and Lever Brothers' which drew their raw materials from colonial sources commonly emphasised imperial connections in their advertising. More generally, food and drink companies frequently wrapped their products and advertised their wares with patriotic and imperial symbols, pursuing their consumers through sentiment as well as by taste, exploiting Britannia, John Bull, the Crown, the Army, the Navy and exotic imperial settings for commercial ends. Even before the First World War a few local 'All British Shopping Weeks' had been organised in defiance of foreign imports, some by a shadowy All-British Shopping Movement formed in 1911, and in the 1920s an emphasis on the British or British Empire quality of various products was common in commercial advertising. The appeal of Shredded Wheat was twofold: 'Britons Make It - It Makes Britons'.[18]

Not surprisingly, therefore, Amery and the EMB turned to experts from outside government service to launch their campaigns. Symptomatic was the appointment to the Board and as vice-chairman of the Publicity Committee of William Crawford, head of one of the two major British advertising agencies in the 1920s. Crawford brought to this work not only his professional experience and ability but also a personal commitment to Empire. 'Everything that is richest and best can be garnered from the soil of the Empire', he wrote. 'All that is needed to sell it is skilled marketing and advertising'. The establishment rewarded his services and his loyalties with a knighthood in 1927. Amery wittily suggested that his KBE stood for 'Keep Buying Empire'.[19] Other outsiders bringing complementary talents to the Publicity Committee included Sir Woodman Burbidge, Chairman and Managing Director of Harrods, Viscount Burnham, President of the Empire Press Union, J.C. Stobart, Director of Education at the BBC and, later, A.P. Ryan, Publicity Manager of the Gas Light and Coke Company. The other outstanding appointment was Frank Pick. Since joining the Metropolitan District Railway in 1906, Pick had engineered a comprehensive transformation of its publicity operations, employing distinguished modern poster artists, typographers and architects and encouraging, criticizing and bullying them to get the best results. He was, it is said, 'the nearest approach to Lorenzo the Magnificent that a modern democracy could achieve'. Promoted to Assistant Managing Director of the combined London Underground and General Omnibus Company in 1921, he was to become Managing Director in 1928 and yet still found the time and energy for his EMB work. It was an obvious but judicious choice to make him chairman of the Publicity Committee's Poster sub-committee.[20]

The operations of the EMB owed much, however, to one remarkable insider, the civil servant Stephen Tallents. He had been involved in the administration of food rationing during the First World War, served on the postwar relief commission in the Baltic provinces, acted later as Imperial Secretary in Northern Ireland and most recently as secretary to the Cabinet Committee dealing with the General Strike. It is possible that those experiences had made him unusually sensitive to the need to assess and massage public opinion. He was hand-picked by Amery to be Secretary to the Empire Marketing Board. In office, he effectively translated the message of the advertising profession into a language of government service. He recognized that in a modern mass democracy, in which the functions of government were increasing, departments of state would be obliged to use publicity as a managerial tool, to keep the public informed, to explain government operations and to obtain public consent by persuasion. He was both stimulated by the likes of Crawford and Pick and helped realise their aspirations in the work of the EMB, not least in its poster campaign. The Times obituarist later described him with unintentional irony as 'An Imaginative Civil Servant'.[21]

Commissioning and Designing

Although the poster campaign was a major part of the EMB's publicity operations, it is important to recognise that this programme supported, and was reinforced by, a wide range of other activities. The EMB was a multi-media event. Each year the Board's specially-designed pavilion appeared at exhibitions throughout the country, like the Ideal Home Exhibition, and each year local retailers responded to the Board's encouragement and organised Empire Shopping Weeks. Each year the Board employed lecturers to spread the message among Women's Institutes, working-men's clubs and similar organisations, and each year the Board continued its experiments in the making and showing of films. The Board published an enormous number of leaflets and reports, many distributed free of charge, and managed without difficulty to persuade the BBC to give it access to the airwaves. Until late in its career the Board was much preoccupied with the designing and placing of press advertisements, and it was not above staging publicity stunts such as the ceremonial cooking of a seven-feet high Empire Christmas Pudding. (For the recipe see Fig. 1.) But it was the poster campaign, costing altogether £426,879, which eventually absorbed the largest share of the Publicity Committee's budget and which attracted most public discussion.[22]

The importance attached to the poster campaign may be judged by the attention given to it at the first meeting of the newly-constituted Publicity Committee on 8th July 1926: 'It was agreed that a scheme of poster display...would form a suitable basis for the Board's initial publicity work'.[23] The planning and launching of this campaign were at once handed over to a small sub-committee,[24] and this group was to run the operation thereafter, reporting back to the Publicity Committee and ultimately to the Board for approval. Whereas the Board and the Publicity Committee settled down into usually monthly meetings, the Poster sub-committee maintained a remarkably busy schedule, assembling initially once a week, later once a fortnight, usually in the evening, year after year until the summer of 1931 when more informal arrangements were adopted.

This hum of activity reflected the energetic chairmanship of Frank Pick. Those who worked with him acknowledged his inspiration and leadership,[25] and the detailed records of the sub-committee support their recollections, showing him rarely absent from meetings, taking initiatives, closely supervising all aspects of the poster campaign. Frank McDougall,

FIG. 1   F.C. Harrison, The Empire Christmas Pudding, 25 ins. × 40 ins., displayed November-December 1928, printer Roberts and Leete Ltds., London, EMB ref. A02, PRO ref. CO 956/63.

THE EMPIRE CHRISTMAS PUDDING

according to the recipe supplied by the King's Chef Mr. CEDARD, with Their Majesties' Gracious Consent

1 lb	Currants	Australia
1 lb	Sultanas	Australia or South Africa
1 lb	Stoned Raisins	Australia or South Africa
5 ozs	Minced Apple	United Kingdom or Canada
1 lb	Bread Crumbs	United Kingdom
1 lb	Beef Suet	United Kingdom
6½ ozs	Cut Candied Peel	South Africa
8 ozs	Flour	United Kingdom
8 ozs	Demerara Sugar	British West Indies or British Guiana
5	Eggs	United Kingdom or Irish Free State
½ oz	Ground Cinnamon	India or Ceylon
¼ oz	Ground Cloves	Zanzibar
¼ oz	Ground Nutmegs	British West Indies
¼ teaspoon	Pudding Spice	India or British West Indies
¼ gill	Brandy	Australia · S. Africa Cyprus or Palestine
½ gill	Rum	Jamaica or British Guiana
1 pint	Beer	England · Wales · Scotland or Ireland

WRITE TO THE EMPIRE MARKETING BOARD, WESTMINSTER, FOR A FREE BOOKLET ON EMPIRE CHRISTMAS FARE GIVING THIS AND OTHER RECIPES.

the Australian High Commissioner and representative on the Board, was another assiduous and effective member, and Crawford also either attended sub-committee meetings or aided and encouraged from his dominant position on the Publicity Committee. The sub-committee was otherwise dependent on the contributions of enthusiastic, involved and increasingly knowledgeable civil service officers, especially Tallents who was normally present at the weekly meetings and Gervas Huxley who also held the strategic post of secretary to the Publicity Committee.

The sub-committee rapidly decided on the methods of poster publicity which it would adopt. In the first instance posters would be commissioned for display on existing commercial hoardings, and plans were made to book sites in major cities to take large designs, 20 feet by 10 feet, technically known as 48-sheet size. The first was to be MacDonald Gill's 'Highways of Empire' map of the world, unveiled to considerable acclaim on New Year's Day 1927 (reproduced from a smaller scale version as Plate 1).[26] But the cost of this method and the prohibition on the display of posters of such dimensions by some cities meant that only one other design of this size followed, in March 1927 (by F.C. Herrick),[27] and the decision was then taken to shift to a series of 16-sheet posters, 80 inches by 120 inches in size. Over subsequent years, a few of these, probably no more than seven designs, appeared on commercial hoardings, and though they included work by McKnight Kauffer and Austin Cooper, they appear to have provoked little comment.[28] Much more sustained was the provision of special publicity material for retailers, for regular use in shops or in lavish displays during local Empire Shopping Weeks. Judging mainly from surviving copies, at least 32 designs were issued as shop window bills, several printed in a variety of sizes ranging from 20 inches by 30 inches to 5 inches by $7\frac{1}{2}$ inches, some re-issued with alternative wordings.[29] (For one example, by Horace Taylor, see picture on the back cover.) Some designs were also printed on stiffer material as a series of shop window cards and at least 28 further designs were issued in this form, again in a wide variety of sizes.[30] Another sequence incorporating at least another 24 different designs was displayed as shop window strips varying from 50 inches to 20 inches in length.[31] It appears that the EMB even commissioned labels for use on Empire tinned products.[32] Another proposal adopted by the sub-committee led to the designing of 32 contract posters for display in factories making goods for export to the overseas Empire,[33] and a similar idea was to produce half a dozen contract labels printed on paper and on card for affixing to goods being exported to India and each of the dominions.[34]

However, the EMB attracted most attention by displaying its posters on its own specially-designed wooden-framed hoardings erected in public places. The idea for this campaign appears to have been Pick's. The frames were some twenty-five feet in length and about five feet high, and they were placed on solus sites, therefore detached from ordinary commercial advertising and consequently more dignified and eye-catching. Five posters were to be shown on each frame, made up of two outer panels and one central panel each 60 inches by 40 inches and two inner panels each 25 inches by 40 inches. Here Pick was incorporating poster sizes with which he was familiar from his London Underground experience. The novelty was to conceive of the five posters displayed as a single linked concept. They were bound together by a sixth letter press strip, 65 inches by $5\frac{3}{4}$ inches, carrying a top caption (see Fig. 2). Initially the three larger panels were intended to carry pictorial posters and the two smaller to contain letter press messages aimed at the public, but flexibility soon produced such variants as five pictorial posters or a single graphic design stretching across the entire display. All the plates reproduced in this volume are taken from the frame poster sequences. The first set (including Plate 4) appeared in January 1927, and thereafter the sub-committee aimed to change the display normally after three weeks and from early 1931 after four weeks. Some designs were reissued, but altogether probably a hundred different sets were commissioned by Pick's sub-committee and displayed on the frames during the lifetime of the EMB.[35]

The particular conviction which Pick, and also Crawford, brought to the business of commissioning the posters to fill these frames was the belief that only designs of high aesthetic quality delivered their publicity message effectively. Not only did good design give pleasure, but because of that it had the greatest public impact. Good design was not an optional extra, but essential to achieve the EMB's purpose. It was necessary to 'move the hearts and minds', to 'touch the imagination of the people', by 'bringing the

FIG. 2 E. McKnight Kauffer, One Third of the Empire is in the Tropics, displayed September-October 1927, printer Haycock, Cadle and Graham Ltd., London, EMB refs. N1-N5 and top N, PRO refs. CO 956/499-504. Illustration of posters on frame hoardings from *Commercial Art* vol.4, February 1928, p.45.

Empire alive'.[36] Moreover, the dignity of a government operation required the pictorial content, graphic design and lettering of the posters to be of superior quality.[37] The selection of artists and the commissioning of designs were therefore of critical importance.

As the poster campaign developed Pick's committee consequently became a major patron of commercial art and inevitably the recipient of specimens of work submitted by artists eager to receive commissions. Several applicants seem to have been rejected brusquely out of hand,[38] although a group of West African art students from Achimota were at least fobbed off with a water colour painting set each.[39] It was perhaps unfortunate that 'the sub-committee also considered examples of Mr. Graham Sutherland's work, but did not feel that there was any opportunity for utilising this artist'.[40] The names of some artists who contacted the Board were noted for possible future reference,[41] and a few sufficiently impressed Pick and the committee to receive commissions in due course, including Barnard Lintott (Plate 15), Austin Cooper (Plate 20), Kenneth Shoesmith (Plate 31) and Guy Kortright (Plate 34).[42] But for the most part the sub-committee appear to have taken the initiative, to have kept the available talent under constant review, and to have issued invitations as needed to artists it approved.

Not all those whose names were noted by the committee received invitations and not all those who were asked accepted commissions. C.R. Nevinson, Duncan Grant, Laura Knight, C.F. Tunnicliffe, Ben Nicholson, Eric Ravilious and others appear in the records as possibilities but it is doubtful if they were ever formally approached. Pick contacted Edward Wadsworth without success, and Philip Connard appears not to have been persuaded to produce a still life design in spite of an offer of 150 guineas. Rex Whistler was much pursued but never apparently landed, being variously invited to produce shop window bills and a set of frame posters illustrating 'John Bull's Empire Breakfast Table'.[43] Perhaps the most disappointing episode was the sub-committee's failure to agree on the artist suitable to produce an apparently much-desired humorous poster. 'Poy' of the Evening News was considered at one stage, Low at another. Crawford suggested inviting John Hassall but the 'Sub-Committee felt...that Mr. Hassall's qualifications were not suitable for the designing of work for the Board'. In fact Hassall did produce a sketch, but this was rejected by the committee as inappropriate. By this decision, Hassall was denied an opportunity to do for the British Empire what he had done for Skegness.[44]

Not surprisingly many of those employed by the EMB, especially in the early stages of the campaign, had previously produced work for Pick's London Underground. These included MacDonald Gill whose 'Wonderground' map was a forerunner of the many maps commissioned by the EMB, beginning with his massive 'Highways of Empire' (Plates 1 and 54). New designs were also commissioned from E.A. Cox (Plate 5), Spencer Pryse (Plates 10, 12, 29 and 30), Fred Taylor (Plates 11, 14, 50 and 52), Horace Taylor (back cover), Charles Pears (Plates 6, 22-26, 59 and 60), and perhaps most famously from E. McKnight Kauffer whose first design for

Pick in 1915 began an extraordinary sequence of exciting modernist designs which revealed a talent Pick was anxious to enroll for the work of the EMB (Plates 16-18 and Fig. 2).[45]

Sometimes other members of the EMB would propose artists for consideration. A member of the staff visited an exhibition of British artists at Liverpool and returned with one or two names, and it was the same officer who persuaded the sub-committee that it was worth visiting the Imperial Institute to see the friezes being painted by Edgar Ainsworth. A commission resulted (Plates 55 and 56a).[46] The Irish Free State representative on the Board, always anxious to ensure that the products of that dominion were sufficiently publicised, successfully recommended Margaret Clarke to the sub-committee.[47] Apparently in an effort to encourage new talent, Pick's group invited applications from the nation's art schools. A few label designs emanated from these sources, and Mr. Suddaby from the Leeds School of Arts was honoured by a commission for a set of frame posters.[48] A competition organised by the Royal Society of Arts to produce a design for the EMB attracted 140 entries.[49]

Occasionally the theme to be illustrated on the poster frames was proposed from outside Pick's committee. The Ministry of Agriculture's National Marks campaign was helped along by EMB posters in 1927, and their obligations to British farmers were backed by a milk publicity operation in 1928.[50] It was at the request of the British Trawlers' Federation and partly using their money that Charles Pears was commissioned to design an 'Eat More Fish' sequence of posters (Plates 59 and 60), and Adrian Allinson's commission followed a letter to the Board from the East Africa Trade Commissioner (Plates 48 and 49).[51] But usually the sub-committee took the initiative and planned its own programme. It was indeed normal for them to decide upon a subject or theme, and then to select the appropriate artist. For example, the decision to launch the poster campaign with a special Empire map was taken before MacDonald Gill was consulted (Plate 1), and the theme of air communications was discussed before Pat Keely was approached (Plate 2b).[52] Sir William Nicholson had to be persuaded to tackle the theme of an Empire nursery breakfast table, and the idea of a poster on the subject of the Empire Christmas Pudding originated with the committee and not with the artist who executed the commission, F.C. Harrison (Plate 36). Once the idea of a set illustrating home agriculture was agreed, Clare Leighton was contacted as the artist most suitable to execute it (Plate 37).[53] Frank Pick proposed a whole batch of posters illustrating reciprocity of trade between Britain and the overseas Empire, and then set about choosing the artists (Plates 45-7 and 56b). In planning a further set, highlighting the dates at which various commodities had first been imported into Britain from the Empire, the secretariat was set to work researching the facts some time before an artist was chosen and given the material to work on (Plate 53).[54]

Sometimes the instructions given to the artist were extraordinarily precise. Frank Pape was required to follow closely the sub-committee's own ideas and design the edges of his tobacco posters to make them look like the labels of cigar boxes (Plates 39-41).[55] The Palestine set was to show in its three scenes the River Jordan with almond trees in blossom, Jerusalem with sheep and olives, and Mount Carmel in the background with Jaffa oranges: Frank Newbould followed this brief closely (Plate 44). The Board received from A.A. Moore and Irene Fawkes precisely what the sub-committee ordered for their bulbs set, three large illustrations of scenes in the Isles of Scilly, Lincolnshire and Cornwall and two smaller designs displaying bouquets of flowers (Plate 38).[56] Newbould was asked to design a centrepiece 'on the subject of the Empire builders who have no memorial. It was suggested that this might take the form of a pioneer clearing virgin country' (Plate 51).[57] Of course, some artists interpreted their instructions rather more independently. Kerr Lawson, for example, produced final designs for Armistice Day 1929 radically different from the sub-committee's original vision and indeed from the artist's own first sketches. No wonder Gervas Huxley, who was sent down to inspect the nearly completed work in Kerr Lawson's studio, reported that Pick should see it as soon as possible: fortunately the result satisfied everyone (Plate 3a).[58]

This episode is a reminder of how much control the sub-committee tried to exercise over the artists as they worked. It was invariably the case that artists were expected to offer sketches of the designs they had been commissioned to produce for the critical examination of Pick and his colleagues. This was never a formality. It was often the start of a sometimes prolonged series of exchanges. The famous 'Highways of Empire' map was very different from the original pencil sketch prepared by MacDonald Gill. The Mercator projection he first employed was regarded by the sub-committee as an inappropriate shape for reproduction on a 48-sheet poster. The idea of the eventual lunette shape was finally evolved by Pick following suggestions made by McDougall, Tallents and Huxley. The cartographers George Philip and Son then drew the projection in outline for Gill to use in his design. (The inclusion of polar bears at the South Pole was a mistake noticed only at proofs stage and this explains why at the suggestion of Tallents the poor beasts are made to inquire 'Where are we?')[59]

Many other designs were also amended, though for less entertaining reasons. Occasionally, outsiders with specialist knowledge of the subject matter would be consulted to ensure technical accuracy. Clive Gardiner's electrical machinery design (Plate 9) was put to the General Electricity Company, and McKnight Kauffer's cocoa sketch (Plate 16) was shown to the Gold Coast Trade Commissioner.[60] Our curiosity about the nature of Adrian Allinson's original design for one poster is aroused when we read that 'the whip in the hand of the large figure' was removed at the request of the East Africa Trade Commissioner (Plate 49).[61] But the sub-committee was the source of most changes. They decided to reduce the number of figures assembled by Fred Taylor as Empire Builders (Plates 50 and 52), changed part of Gregory Brown's Australian cattle-raising scene (Plate 13), and required modification in McKnight Kauffer's banana palms design (Plate 18).[62] Gossop's Australian trade sequence (Plate 2a) caused prolonged

trouble, and F.C. Harrison's set intended for Christmas 1927 ran into such a critical barrage that after repeated amendments it was found acceptable for display only for the following season.[63] Barnard Lintott was clearly in trouble when the sub-committee minuted that one of his Canadian designs was approved but 'in regard to the two others it was arranged that in the first instance further particulars should be obtained from the artist as to what these designs depicted'.[64]

At least Lintott salvaged his commission. Not everyone did. Hugh Williams produced an acceptable rough design for the sub-committee in August 1927, but only one poster of his set was printed, though not displayed, and his commission was cancelled in July 1930 after much unsuccessful labour.[65] Harold Nelson struggled from March 1928 to April 1929 with a commission intended for Armistice Day but was then dismissed.[66] Service Advertising Studio also had problems with their Christmas set: they were offered the commission early in 1929, were sent repeatedly back to the drawing board by the sub-committee, were threatened with dismissal in June 1929 and finally lost the contract in January 1930.[67] Perhaps the most surprising indication of the rigour of Pick and the sub-committee was their treatment of Spencer Pryse whose distinguished record in the poster world did not protect him from tough criticism. His first Indian rice fields design was subjected to severe criticism by the Indian representative on the Board and by others who saw it, apparently for technical inaccuracy. He was obliged to abandon it and begin afresh, using photographs provided to guide him and subjecting his sketch to the scrutiny of the sub-committee (Plate 10).[68] The Gold Coast designs he brought back from a West African tour were also criticised by the sub-committee and amended (Plates 29 and 30), and he was asked to subject for examination by the sub-committee his cartoons for a Nigeria set because the first set 'fell below the standard of draftsmanship which they were entitled to expect and it was agreed that Mr. Spencer Pryse should be officially notified to this effect'. He later offered to design a third set based upon his West African sketches, but the proposal was rejected.[69]

The firmness with which artists were treated generally reflected the critical certainty of Pick. His tended to be the dominant mind and personality at those evening sub-committee meetings. In his memoirs, Tallents recorded Pick at work, leaving some artists to follow their own inspirations, laying down subject and treatment to others, sometimes dogmatically.[70] On the rare occasions when Pick was not present to make a decision, the minutes tend to record conclusions taken 'subject to Mr. Pick's approval'. Only on one occasion does Pick not seem to have had his own way. When the unfortunate Mr. Nelson lost his commission to produce a frame set for Armistice Day 1929 the sub-committee decided in May 1929 to approach Stanley Spencer. It was rare for Spencer to accept commissions and he himself expressed doubts as to his suitability. Pick, however, was enthusiastic, perhaps persuaded and excited by the originality of the artist. Within three weeks Spencer had produced rough sketches. Pick acknowledged that they were not designs suitable for an Armistice Day set, but he was clearly much impressed by the work. On his own authority he commissioned Spencer to complete the sequence and promised that the posters, when finished, would be displayed on the Board's frames. But the sub-committee members as a whole were evidently less certain when in August they saw the finished designs. Was it the curious subject matter of the five pictures, 'The Art Class', 'The Hat Stand', 'The Anthracite Stove', 'Cutting the Cloth', and 'The Garage', or the idiosyncratic visionary treatment of these topics which made Pick's colleagues unsure about their suitability as designs appropriate for the Empire Marketing Board? Other members of the Publicity Committee appear to have been consulted. Though the designs were formally approved, and paid for, their display was deferred indefinitely until a 'suitable opportunity offered'. Pick was indignant at the rebuff, which constituted a rare challenge to his judgement.[71]

The importance of good design to Pick's sub-committee is indicated by the fees which they were prepared to pay to extract commissions from artists they wanted. As a standard of comparison, it is worth recalling that £250 a year was regarded between the wars as a top wage for a skilled manual worker. In the late 1920s you could buy a new two-reception three-bedroom semi in Greater London for around £700 and could park in front of it the latest Morris Minor saloon for £135. It is true that small commissions such as a shop window bill could cost as little as 10 guineas, and Horace Taylor's 'Follow the Empire Makers' (back cover) at 20 guineas was regarded as the maximum for this kind of graphic design.[72] But substantial fees were paid for frame poster designs, varying naturally according to the status of the artist and the complexity of the commission, graphic work generally costing less than pictorial design. The comparatively unknown Mr. Webb from Western Australia was initially offered only 50 guineas for a single poster design (Plate 35), the Burmese artist Ba Nyan 60 guineas for each of his (Plates 27 and 28). Humbert Craig was paid 65 guineas (Plate 57) but George Houston whose work appeared in the same set received 75 guineas.

The latter fee was also paid to John Nash (Plate 32).[73] The exceptional quality and complexity of MacDonald Gill's map designs earned him 150 guineas for each (Plates 1 and 54).[74] It was, of course, financially more attractive to be commissioned to produce a full set of five frame posters, although here too rates of pay varied. Gossop and Keely received £200 for their graphic design sets (Plate 2), H.S. Williamson a more generous £250 (Plate 21) and Austin Cooper as much as £300 for his Christmas set (Plate 20).[75] A group of commissions all dealing with the same theme of the reciprocity of trade between industrial Britain and the overseas Empire were offered to H.S. Williamson for £250 and to Keith Henderson for 250 guineas (Plate 56b), but to Charles Pears and Frank Newbould for 350 guineas (Plates 45 and 46).[76] This last fee was generally offered only to favourite sons: while Clare Leighton was paid £250 for her 'Home Farms' set (Plate 37), Charles Pears received 350 guineas for his 'Highway to India' sequence (Plates 22-26). Clive Gardiner's remarkable set included three pictorial and two graphic and letter press designs and he received 280 guineas for the complete sequence (Plates 7-9).[77]

Artists occasionally queried the fees offered them. Paul Nash accepted his commission for 60 guineas and was rebuffed by the sub-committee when he later asked for £100.[78] Artists forced to make substantial amendments to their designs sometimes asked for a further fee but rarely successfully.[79] Spencer Pryse was an exception. He negotiated a remarkable contract of 1000 guineas for two sets of five posters, and then succeeded in screwing an extra 100 guineas out of the sub-committee to cover yet more of the travel expenses of his West African expedition.[80] McKnight Kauffer also found himself at loggerheads with Pick over fees, in spite of his eminence and their well-established working relationship. 'Mr. Pick informed Mr. Kauffer that the Committee were not prepared to make any revision of his agreed fee' for his tropical Empire set: eventually he received £300 for the complete set and his request for a further 25 guineas was rejected.[81] Stanley Spencer at least received his 300 guineas fee.[82]

Printing and Displaying

Equal pains were taken to ensure a high quality in the printing of the poster designs. The techniques of lithography employed by commercial printers at this time required the artists' original designs to be transferred on to either lithographic stones or in most cases to zinc plates from which they were printed. A few of the artists commissioned by the EMB, such as Spencer Pryse, undertook this critical transfer themselves, for a higher fee of course. Sir William Nicholson accepted £400 for his designs and for personally putting them on to the stones, and Kerr Lawson received 450 guineas for one of his sets (Plate 3a). Adrian Allinson was originally offered £250 for his set but then agreed to put the designs on the stones for a total fee of 500 guineas. Interestingly the sub-committee had ascertained that if the printers undertook this work the cost would be £200 more.[83] In the great majority of cases, however, the transfers were done by the specialist lithographers employed by the printers.

The sub-committee were required to follow normal government practice and had to put orders for printing out to tender through HMSO. At least thirty different firms were employed during the Board's history, mainly in London but also in Nottingham, Edinburgh, Glasgow, Leeds, Leicester and Manchester. Waterlow and Sons received the largest number of contracts and served the sub-committee throughout its existence. Considerable use was also made of Eyre and Spottiswoode and John Horn. The sub-committee generally agreed with HMSO that work should be awarded to the lowest bidder, and on at least one occasion Pick responded to a Waterlow quotation by requiring a reduction.[84] But Pick was also concerned with the quality of the printing. When HMSO opposed the award of a contract to Thomas Forman and Co., the *highest* bidder, the sub-committee insisted on backing their preference since 'it was essential for the Board's special purpose that a standard of printing should be set up for this whole series of animal showcards and they were satisfied that for this object the work could only be safely entrusted to Messrs. Forman'.[85]

The companies chosen for particular commissions were required to be most careful to ensure not only that the designs were faithfully reproduced by the company's lithographers but that the colouring was also exact. The work was sometimes very difficult. The design of MacDonald Gill's 'Highways of Empire' map (Plate 1) had to be photographed and blown up to four times the original size as the basis for the lithograph, and this emphasised certain blemishes in the original drawing which were only 'got over by a

considerable quantity of hard work'.[86] Paul Nash sketched his market gardening design in chalk and this had to be printed as rapidly as possible, perhaps before it blew away.[87] Mark Gertler delivered as requested three entirely acceptable designs, 'Spring', 'Summer' and 'Autumn', for £100 each, but the sub-committee had to accept 'that the ordinary standard of printing would be quite inadequate to procure an effective reproduction of the designs', and more sophisticated techniques were ruled out on the grounds of expense.[88] The sub-committee also experimented with the use of photographs in poster designs. A crisis occurred when one picture intended for a milk publicity display went wrong, and Tallents had to improvise rapidly: to provide a substitute, he photographed his own children sitting at home on a log clutching glasses of milk served by the family maid.[89]

In all cases, the companies were required to submit proofs of their work for the scrutiny of the sub-committee. While most appear to have been acceptable, amendments, for example to the tone of colours, were not infrequently demanded. The gold used in Gossop's design (Plate 2a) seems to have caused particular trouble. Some proofs submitted by John Waddington were regarded as so unsatisfactory that fresh proofs were demanded, and Caustons were told to submit a re-proof, 'accurate as regards scale and colouring', or lose their contract. Occasionally, further inadequacies appeared only after proofs found acceptable had been printed. Waterlow's printing of a shop window card was deemed to be so bad that the sub-committee obliged the company to knock twenty per cent off their bill.[90] Vincent Brooks Day practically withdrew from the EMB's business after one savaging, complaining that the poor printing of posters they had handled (including Plate 4) was because they were obliged to quote low and use plates and rotary printing machines rather than the more expensive stones and flat bed presses upon which they henceforth insisted.[91] Gervas Huxley claimed in 1928 that as a result of the sub-committee's criticisms, 'we are I think gradually getting printers to realise that they have got to pay particular attention to our work'.[92] It might also be noted in this context that Pick naturally insisted on bringing to the EMB's posters the high-quality lettering which had been incorporated in his London Underground commissions: the Board did, indeed, adopt the same Johnston sans serif type fount for use on its posters, and later commissioned from Stanley Morison of the Lanston Monotype Corporation another design upon which Eric Gill was engaged.[93]

Once the proofs had been approved by the sub-committee the posters could be run off by offset printing machines, producing perhaps 1,000 copies an hour.[94] Around 3,000 copies of Macdonald Gill's 48-sheet world map were printed. Usually 2,000 copies of each of the early frame posters were required. The costs inevitably varied owing to the company and perhaps especially the number of colours required to produce the tones needed in the design. Herrick's New Zealand design (Plate 4) cost £145.15s.0d. to print, Cox's sugar cane picture (Plate 5) £191.16s.10d. and the Suez Canal design by Charles Pears (Plate 6) £161.2s.5d. The letter press designs were, of course, cheaper to print, so that the total cost of printing 2,000 copies of the first set of frame posters amounted to £479.3s.8d. and 2,000 copies of the second set £647.9s.7d. Costs obviously increased when, later, longer print runs were ordered.[95]

When the posters had been printed they had, of course, to be distributed and displayed. The EMB secretariat was involved in booking hoarding sites, getting its own frames erected and maintained, employing billposters and appointing inspectors to ascertain that the work had been properly done. Pick, once again, was meticulous in arranging these practical details, backed as usual by Tallents and his team. Initially, 1500 sites were booked for three months in 1927 for the 48-sheet poster campaign (the cost was first estimated at £7,800 for 1,000 sites), and when this programme ended, another £15,000 was set aside to book hoarding space for a 20-week 16-sheet campaign covering seaside resorts and towns with populations of over 50,000 people.[96] At the same time the sub-committee was beginning to persuade retail grocers to accept and display the shop window bills, cards and strips that the EMB was offering. The 3200 grocers on its lists in the autumn of 1928 rose rapidly thereafter, and according to Tallents over 7 million shop window posters were eventually printed for retailers to display.[97] Likewise, the number of firms displaying the EMB's contract posters in their factories increased from 100 late in 1928 to 800 by September 1929.[98] Most conspicuous, however, was the increase in the number of frame poster hoardings, already reaching 1,000 by December 1927 and concluding with 1,800 sites in 450 towns by 1933. Their erection, often on sites never before used for advertising purposes, required careful negotiation with local authorities, private owners, railway companies and others. The Secretary of State wrote to Lord Mayors and Lord Provosts around the country endeavouring to persuade them to allow the EMB's hoardings to be sited on municipal property. The cost of the construction work was closely monitored by the sub-committee, and it succeeded in obtaining sites either free of charge or at low rents, between £10 and £50 a year. Inevitably, Pick paid attention to the very woodwork of the hoardings erected, English oak or British Columbian pine, requiring the wooden strips between the panels on the first frames erected to be slimmed down and the colour of the wood staining to be altered.[99]

The sub-committee also found other ways of displaying and distributing the poster designs and with them their message. As part of a special Buy British campaign in November 1931, launched in the economic crisis, four million copies in varying sizes of two posters specially designed by Austin Cooper and Tom Purvis were issued via local offices of the Ministry of Labour, local authorities, Boy Scouts groups, in house to house distribution and by other means, and were displayed on hoardings, on walls, in shops, in offices, on motor cars....[100] EMB posters naturally appeared at EMB exhibitions, but less obviously in the waiting rooms of Labour Exchanges.[101] Commercial companies were also attracted by the designs and the EMB was willing to authorise their use, by Messrs. John Dickinson and Co. as covers

to some of their stationery, by Messrs. Jones & Co. as pictures for jigsaws, by Messrs. George Philip and Son Ltd. as designs for an Empire card game.[102] Eight designs were reprinted in 5,000 sets by the EMB itself, and issued as Christmas cards, and twelve of its designs were reissued as postcards.[103] MacDonald Gill's much reproduced 'Highways of Empire' map was printed in miniature, and an astonishing 26,000 copies were distributed by the EMB at the Schoolboy's Own Exhibition in 1929. Perhaps inspired by that success, the sub-committee also decided to print 250,000 sets in cigarette card sizes of Herrick's attractive animal designs (Plate 43).[104]

Such products were, of course, aimed at children. It is apparent that the EMB devoted considerable attention to ways of impressing its message upon the young. The Publicity Committee decided at its second meeting in July 1926 to explore the possibilities for publicity work in schools. Thereafter many of the lectures and film shows arranged by the Board were aimed at school audiences and some of its publications were for their consumption.[105] The Poster sub-committee was also involved from the beginning in this kind of activity. In November 1926 Crawford suggested that the reproduction of some posters for schools, and the general public, 'might form the basis of effective propaganda'.[106] Initially the sub-committee merely responded to the requests which it began to receive from schoolteachers and the general public for copies of the frame posters which caught their attention. MacDonald Gill's 'Highways of Empire' map generated 300 letters, mainly from schools, within two months of its first display.[107] To begin with, spare copies of the posters were distributed, but very soon it was decided to reprint selected designs on more robust paper and sometimes in a smaller size, usually 30 inches by 20 inches.[108] Thirteen designs were reprinted in 1929-30, for example, and eleven in 1930-31.[109] Posters were sold to the general public, those 60 inches by 40 inches costing three shillings and sixpence, those 30 inches by 20 inches a mere one shilling and sixpence, but they were given free of charge to schools.[110] EMB staff were conscious that pressing their propaganda material on schools might be resented, but more discreetly, by letting teachers know that material was freely available, they ensured the build-up of an astonishing amount of demand. A letter which Tallents placed in *The Times* in September 1927 accelerated inquiries. There were 9,000 requests from schools for copies of EMB posters in the Board's first year of operation, and by May 1933 there were 27,000 schools on its mailing list in regular receipt of new posters, the vast majority of the schools in Britain, ranging from elementary schools to Eton. To add to their value as teaching aids, the Board also issued accompanying leaflets, written by John Buchan, Henry Newbolt and others.[111] Interestingly, the quality of the posters for teaching purposes was recognised by the publishers Macmillan who obtained permission to use twenty-five EMB posters in a collection of pictures which it issued in 1932 for use in geography lessons and which went into a fourth reprint in 1939.[112]

The Message

The efforts which the sub-committee made to impress its message on the young suggest that the Empire Marketing Board was concerned not only with influencing the imperial consumers of today but also with moulding the minds of the imperial citizens and consumers of tomorrow. The EMB and the Poster sub-committee were, indeed, consciously engaged in the dissemination of propaganda, a word they did not shy away from using.

What was the message, then, which the EMB and especially the posters were intended to express? It is necessary to notice first that although it was the Board's job to publicise the food and agricultural products of the Empire, they were not seeking to extol specific branded commodities: that was for commercial companies or colonial producers and governments to do. The sub-committee began its campaigns by attempting to follow closely the publicity concept laid down by the Board and aimed to illustrate only very broad imperial themes in its work. It was initially reluctant to emphasise the particular commodities of named countries. This limitation was, however, difficult to follow and was soon eroded, generating occasional pangs of concern among members of the Publicity Committee and Poster sub-committee.[113] Indeed, one poster sequence which incorporated pictures of a particular brand of New Zealand honey in its design was printed but then abandoned and never displayed, probably on the grounds that it was too particular in its content.[114] Essentially, the EMB was advancing general claims about the Empire. It was engaged, as Tallents later put it, 'in the mobilisation and distribution of ideas'. Against this background, commercial companies and colonial governments could set their own more specific publicity.[115] Moreover, as befitted a propaganda operation, especially one aimed at the masses, the ideas mobilised by the Board and Poster sub-committee were simple, readily comprehensible, and much repeated.

It was, for example, much emphasised in the poster campaign that the British Empire included the United Kingdom as well as the overseas Empire. As noted, the EMB had been committed to publicising home food products because of the lobbying by British farmers and the Ministry of Agriculture, but this obligation allowed the Board to insist in consequence that Britain was part of the Empire and that British citizens were unavoidably members of an imperial society: there was no place for Little Englanders. The concept was neatly implied on the posters by a much-used slogan 'Buy Empire Goods from Home and Overseas' (Plate 1 and back cover).[116] Moreover, citizens of the Empire, at home and overseas, were bound by an especial intimacy: 'The Empire is One Large Family', proclaimed one poster, 'Keep Trade in the Family', urged another, 'Remember the Empire, Filled with your Cousins', advised a third. Here were natural ties: 'You are Partners in an Empire   Make it Prosperous'.[117]

The size of this Empire received inevitable and impressive emphasis: 'The British Empire at Home and Beyond the Seas offers you the resources of A QUARTER OF THE WORLD'.[118] The Poster sub-committee took pains to ensure that publicity was given to the large number of individual territories which made up this single family. Several poster sequences portrayed the products of the United Kingdom and inevitably those of the white dominions of New Zealand, Australia, South Africa, Canada and the Irish Free State. India too figured frequently, and also Ceylon, and one sequence dealt with the new Middle Eastern possessions. A veritable roll call of territories within the Colonial Empire paraded month by month across the frames. The territorial extent and wide variety explained the enormous range of Empire products available for the privileged British consumer, and the poster artists were commissioned to provide the images to illustrate that message. Each territory appeared to offer its own tribute, the harvest from the land in the British Isles plus fresh fish from the sea, flowers from Scilly, vegetables from the Channel Islands. New Zealand offered wool and dairy products, wheat came from Canada, sugar from Mauritius, tea from Ceylon, oranges from South Africa, cocoa from the Gold Coast, cotton from the Sudan, tobacco from Nyasaland, pineapples from Malaya, even arrowroot from tiny St. Vincent. Not only was Burma 'the rice granary of the world', but an amazed British public learned that its annual exports were sufficient to make 'THIRTY-TWO THOUSAND MILLION RICE PUDDINGS'.[119] Great Britain was a shop in which the commodities of an imperial world were always available and on display (Plates 11 and 21). One image employed on the posters and in other EMB publicity operations was the Christmas pudding, an Empire Christmas Pudding, a rich and appetising globe composed entirely from Empire ingredients (fig. 1 and Plate 36). That impression of a self-contained and self-sufficient world was reinforced by other slogans on the posters, which announced specifically, for example, that 'The Empire can Grow its own Cotton', that 'The Empire grows enough tea to supply all the Empire's needs' and more generally that 'The Empire supplies our every Need'.[120]

Moreover, this appeared to be a structured and highly centralised Empire. Many posters depicted the lines of communication under British control which guided these flows of Empire trade safely into British hands and homes. Central to the vision were the sea routes binding the Empire together (Plate 1). They were joined by the air and cable routes and wireless stations spreading across Pat Keely's five-poster strip with its top caption 'Speed Empire Trade' (Plate 2b). Vivid images of the Channel, the Mersey, the Suez Canal, 'The Empire's Highway to India' and the ports of the Empire overseas reinforced the message (Plates 6, 19, 22-26 and 31).

The integration of the Empire implied by such pictures was coupled with a stress on the mutual dependence between the Empire at home and the Empire overseas. The prosperity of one depended upon and fuelled the prosperity of the other (Plate 2a). It was common to show on the posters in simple statistical terms how Britain's best customers were apparently in the overseas Empire since they bought more British exports per head than did foreigners. For example: 'On the average every person in the Irish Free State bought in 1928 nearly £12 worth of U.K. products. The highest average among our principal foreign customers was less than £3 per head'. It paid, then, to 'Support Your Best Customers' and to 'Keep Your Money in the Empire' by buying Empire products, thus increasing Empire purchasing power (Plates 23 and 25).[121] This theme led, more specifically, to a stress on the interdependence between the manufacturing sector of the British imperial economy and its agricultural sector. Still more precisely, it meant emphasising the interdependence between the United Kingdom's manufacturing sector and the rest of the Empire, since overseas territories were categorised solely as primary producers. A natural harmony between these sectors was happily assumed to exist. While it was pointed out that already a large share of Britain's manufactured goods was exported to the overseas Empire, it was also argued that the way to increase the volume of those exports was to buy the food products of the overseas Empire. 'Empire Buying Makes Busy Factories' was a theme much illustrated, for example in sequences which coupled apple orchards in Canada with shipbuilding in the United Kingdom, Indian tea and Lancashire cotton, South African fruit and British electrical engineering, dairying in Australia and steel manufacturing in the United Kingdom (Plates 45 and 46).[122] The posters which the EMB specifically designed for display in British factories announced that a contract for the overseas Empire was currently in hand in this factory and continued:

'Question: How can you help to secure further contracts from the Empire?
Answer: By buying, and by getting your wife to buy, the produce that the Empire sends us.'[123]

The advantages of such discriminating purchasing for employment prospects in Britain were, of course, made apparent. It was a commonplace at this time to claim that imperial development and trade would relieve the unemployment endemic in the 1920s and 1930s, and the posters reminded the public to 'Buy British, Create Employment', 'Remember the Unemployed, They are Your Brothers'. Here, then, was an appeal to the enlightened self-interest of the British consumer, an emphasis on the utility of Empire.[124]

Of course, in reality, the Empire was not economically self-sufficient, and British imports and exports still depended on foreign customers and suppliers. That explains why so much weight was placed by the EMB on the untapped potential of the overseas Empire and on the work of development that was needed and that was taking place. Posters, for example, illustrated forest clearance in Canada, the opening up of 'Virgin

Lands' in Australia and road and bridge construction in East Africa (Plates 48 and 49).[125] One caption reads: 'Jungles Today are Gold Mines Tomorrow' (Plate 17). The forces which would accelerate this programme were also clearly identified: British consumers. 'Buy and Build', they were told. 'Empire Buyers are Empire Builders', 'Empire Buying means Empire Building', 'Every Empire Buyer an Empire Builder', the slogans repeated the theme.[126] The EMB's propaganda aimed to flatter British consumers into Empire consciousness by persuading them that their daily purchases were pressing forward the development of a new imperial world. The Empire's destiny lay in the hands of the people. Their decisions, not those of politicians, would, seemingly, determine its future.

Similarly, 'Every Empire Worker an Empire Builder'.[127] The role of the producer, especially of the labourer, was also much emphasised. In some posters, workers in the Colonial Empire evidently laboured under the direction of white supervisors (Plates 31, 39 and 41). But essentially this appeared to be a democratic, egalitarian Empire in which labour, by all races, was given an especial dignity through its dedication to a single, admirable imperial purpose. One remarkable sequence of posters by Fred Taylor depicted in its outer panels former imperial heroes from Cabot to Clive and from Cook to Rhodes, an elite renowned for military and political achievements. But the central panel focussed on dockyard workers in Britain, the new 'Empire Builders'. The message was thought important and justified reposting this sequence on the frames three years later with a new centre panel this time showing Canadian lumbermen at work. The inner panels read 'Let us now praise famous men' and also 'And some there be which have no memorial'. The top caption underlined the message: 'The Empire is still in Building' (Plates 14 and 50-52).[128] Heroic figures of labour were highlighted in other sets. They appear like classical figures on a frieze in Cox's muscular sugar pickers from Mauritius (Plate 5), as sturdy rice planters in India and Burma (Plates 10 and 27), and as robust tea pickers in Ceylon (Plate 12). They are gathering cocoa pods in the Gold Coast (Plate 29), tending sheep in England (Plate 37), heaving cargoes in Colombo (Plate 31) and hauling in the catch in the North Sea (Plate 59). This was the people's Empire, hard-working, multi-racial, harmonious, forming a partnership (Plate 40).

This interpretation of the Empire obviously had a moral dimension to it, which was closely allied to another, implicit as much as explicit. Occasionally traditional national symbols were used in poster designs to trigger off traditional patriotic responses, the union jack, flags of Empire, Britannia, John Bull, the British lion. But these were used sparingly (Plates 3b, 20 and 21),[129] and surprisingly the appeal of the monarchy was very rarely exploited.[130] Moreover, traditional late 19th-century imperial images of jingoism and military conquest, the iconography of battle, were significantly avoided. No explicit reference was made in the posters to the potential military advantages of greater imperial economic development and self-sufficiency. Instead, the dominant images are civilian, of pastoral calm, harmonious trade, generous abundance for all. The Empire, it appeared, was a force for peace. It is remarkable that in spite of the ostensibly economic purpose of the EMB, the Poster sub-committee took considerable trouble to commission designs for display on Armistice Day. Thus originated the two distinguished friezes designed by Kerr Lawson. The first depicted with quiet certainty idealised fishing and rural communities, displayed under the caption 'The Empire Stands for Peace'. The second, headed 'Service of Empire', emphasised the multi-racial character and the variety and fertility of the Empire (Plate 3). Stephen Tallents recommended as a slogan to the Publicity Committee 'A Well-Built Empire Means the Peace of the World'. The attempt to harness Empire to the cause of international peace made good sense to propagandists after the First World War.[131]

In sum, what was offered to the British public in the posters was bound to be a selective representation of the nature of the British Empire between the wars. Of course, given the EMB's formal purpose, the Empire's economic characteristics and value were emphasised, and the benefits of the imperial connection to ordinary British consumers and employees were inevitably claimed. But this material goal was legitimised and its self-interest muted by emphases also on the life-enhancing developmental aspect of the imperial mission, the benefits it would bring to all nations and races within the Empire, the natural harmony between the peoples, and the contribution Empire was making to world prosperity and peace.

The Impact

A final question obviously remains. To what extent did the EMB in general and the poster campaign in particular achieve their aims? How far did an organisation so energetically directed succeed in impressing imperial beliefs upon the public and affecting their behaviour?

In grappling with this problem, we need to remember the restraints under which the EMB operated. In the first instance a marked hostility can be discerned elsewhere in the government service to the activities of the Board. This was directed particularly to its propaganda work. It is interesting that when the EMB was wound up in 1933, many of its scientific research and marketing operations continued to be funded by other government bodies: only the explicit propaganda activities were abandoned. In part the hostility to them reflected a distaste for official propaganda generated within government and outside by the excesses committed during the First World War. More profoundly, official propaganda or publicity operations appeared to some as undesirable extensions of the functions of government, pushing it into a more managerial and directive role. The Board ran up against still powerful laissez-faire traditions. Tallents was conscious that the EMB's 'new and more creative conception of government' collided with 'the older view of government as a negative function, preventing the bad rather than promoting the good'. He recalled that the Board 'felt itself sometimes an unwanted child in the Government service', and that 'the feeling was prevalent that we were introducing a discreditable element into Whitehall'.[132] It might, however, be noticed that one legacy of the Board was some shift in official attitudes, indicated by Tallents' appointment in 1933 as head of the GPO's Public Relations department and in 1935 as Controller of Public Relations at the BBC and by his selection later as Director-General of the shadow Ministry of Information. When the ministry was finally established one early director was Frank Pick. Many of the EMB's propaganda techniques were adopted by the Ministry of Information and by its successor the Central Office of Information.[133]

The EMB suffered when this hostility was translated into limited funding. Fixing its annual grant was invariably a subject of acrimonious debate between Chancellors of the Exchequer, wedded to orthodox faith in the virtues of balanced budgets, low taxes and limited government expenditure, and Secretaries of State, especially Amery, seeking to establish and then protect a novel and vulnerable institution. On one occasion Amery caused the premature break-up of a Cabinet meeting by threatening resignation if the cuts demanded in the Board's funding were fully implemented.[134] Select Committees were additionally hostile to the financial independence of the Board and endorsed the Treasury's efforts to tighten control. The severe cyclical downturn in 1929 merely re-emphasised orthodox demands for economies in government expenditure, and indeed in 1931 the Committee on National Expenditure (May Committee) simply proposed the EMB's immediate abolition. While the Board survived, just, that crisis, its funding was further reduced. The Board in fact never received the £1 million a year originally promised. Only £3,681,500 was granted over the eight financial years of its existence, and economy cuts affected all parts of the programme, not least the poster campaign.[135] From early 1931, the Poster sub-committee began to change the frame posters after four weeks instead of after three, it leased some of the hoardings to other government departments, and started to re-use previously displayed posters.[136] The Poster sub-committee itself ceased to exist by the summer, Pick being consulted only informally thereafter. At the end of the year he finally resigned from the Publicity Committee. Soon thereafter other staff were leaving, Huxley, for example, taking his matured talents to the service of the Ceylon Tea Board.[137] As the poster work of the Board was run down, its impact on the public was likely to diminish. In any case we need to compare the £278,414 spent by the Board on publicity at the peak of its activities in 1928 (of which only £92,714 was devoted to the poster campaign) with the estimated £57 million spent altogether on national advertising in Britain that year.[138] Obviously, at no time could the EMB's publicity campaigns monopolise public attention.

The timing of the EMB's abolition was determined, however, not simply by a worsening of the government's financial problem but by the electorate's acceptance in the economic crisis of late 1931 of a National government committed to tariff reform. There followed the signing of imperial preference agreements with the dominions at the Imperial Economic Conference held at Ottawa in July and August 1932. Most enthusiasts for Empire had always regarded tariffs as the more effective method of imperial economic engineering, and for them the Ottawa agreements removed the original explicit *raison d'etre* of the EMB. The need for economy in government expenditure could now prevail. It is ironic that one of the last commissions awarded by the Board was to H.S. Williamson to produce a graphic design for the framed hoardings to celebrate the occasion of the Ottawa Conference.[139] At that meeting the British government announced that the Board would be allowed to lapse in September 1933 unless the dominions governments agreed to share the financial costs. The sum involved was pretty insignificant, but the dominions too preferred tariffs to persuasion. Some, especially the governments of Canada, South Africa and the Irish Free State, also retained a lingering suspicion of a centralised imperial organisation like the EMB which seemed to detract from that national autonomy, albeit within the British Empire, which the dominions between the wars were anxious to assert.[140]

The limited funds granted to the Board and its closure after a comparatively brief existence naturally restricted the impact on the public which Board members intended and expected. But doubts were also expressed at the time about the quality of the posters produced for the Board and about their suitability for the task in hand. Retailers were not apparently impressed by the first shop window bills, and the first designs for the frames displayed with a flourish at the Royal Academy in November 1926 were given a mixed reception. On the whole, *The Times* art critic concluded, they were 'disappointing', it was 'an opportunity missed'. However satisfactory as illustrations, most exhibits lacked 'the concentration in design which is necessary to make an illustration telling in poster form'. *Advertising Weekly* noted the conservatism of most designs and concluded that they were 'not...of much commercial value'. The General Secretary of the British Empire Union decided that they might induce people to emigrate but would not persuade them to buy British. Individual posters were also received unkindly on later occasions, the babies decorating Sir William Nicholson's design for 'Food and Fruits of Empire' being described by one critic as 'disgustingly gross'.[141]

But on balance most observers appear to have seen merit in the designs, and some were welcomed with great enthusiasm. *Commercial Art* published several reviews and was invariably warm in its comments. The German paper *Kosmos* sought permission to reproduce the designs it found so artistically appealing. *The Times*, like many other commentators, had nothing but praise for the McKnight Kauffer designs (Plates 16-18). Kerr Lawson's sequence for Armistice Day 1929 attracted very favourable press comment: H.M. The Queen was moved to write personally to Mrs. Kerr Lawson to offer her congratulations to the artist (Plate 2a).[142] It is true that EMB posters were not on the whole especially innovative in design, as the Metropolitan District Railway's had been, nor did the EMB launch a particular identifiable house style, as Guinness and Shell were to do. Pick instead had chosen a wide range of artists and allowed them to indulge in the natural variety of their styles, mainly pictorial, often graphic. What he attempted to ensure was that they all in their different ways maintained a high aesthetic standard and so had a substantial effect on the public.

It was actually on the grounds of their high artistic quality that the EMB posters were on one occasion criticised. This was, admittedly, by the British Poster Advertising Association, undoubtedly disgruntled by the Board's refusal to use the commercial hoardings which its members controlled. In a lengthy memorandum to the Board in 1929, the Association acknowledged that the designs were often 'delightful', but condemned them as 'unpractical'. They would not affect consumer choice because 'they betray a lack of study of the mass-mind'. They explained that 'Not only are the "masses" - that is to say, the poorer 95 per cent of the population - indifferent to good art, *but they do not understand it*. It is not that they fail to appreciate the merits of a good picture in the modernistic style used by most of the Board's artists. *They don't know what these posters are meant to represent!*' This observation was a rejection of the advertising philosophy of Pick and Crawford, and

unsurprisingly they dismissed the BPAA's criticisms as special pleading (although some members of the Board had earlier expressed similar reservations).[143]

The question raised, however, about the commercial effectiveness of the posters and other publicity schemes was a highly pertinent one, repeatedly asked in the Board and outside. If the purpose of the EMB was to increase the sales of Empire food products at the expense of foreign goods, then surely the efficacy of the operation might be judged by sales figures? Tallents spent much time, especially before Select Committees of the House of Commons, explaining why such calculations were difficult. Frequently the Board relied in its defence on unsolicited testimonials of support received from those who should have been able to judge commercial trends from their own experience, such as the Australian Dried Fruit Board, the Associated Chambers of Commerce of New Zealand, the Association of British Chambers of Commerce and such trade bodies in Britain as the Federation of Grocers' Associations and the Scottish Grocers' Federation. Trade journals like the *Bakers' Record* and the *Fruit, Flower and Vegetable Trade Journal* also sprang to the defence of the Board as did several national newspapers such as the *Financial Times, Manchester Guardian, Irish Times, Glasgow Herald* and especially *The Times*. The Board also made what it could of public response to particular posters, judged mainly by the number of favourable letters received, usually asking for copies, and in a few instances by public reaction to the invitation on some posters to write to the Board for recipes: 3,300 requests for a leaflet on Christmas fare were received within days of Harrison's set being displayed in 1928 (Fig. 1). Officers of the Board even attempted to judge the eye-catching power of MacDonald Gill's world map (Plate 1) by calculating the percentage of people passing a display in Piccadilly Circus who stopped to scrutinize it.[144] In each year of operation, the Board also noted record levels of particular commodities imported into Britain from the overseas Empire, twenty-two records in 1928, for example, twenty-four in 1932, ranging from Australian sultanas and Rhodesian tobacco to Palestinian grapefruit and Malayan canned pineapples.[145] Market research in Britain was still embryonic at this time, but the EMB did attempt to detect changing patterns of consumption by inquiries among selected retailers around the country. The results, made much of by the Board, seemed to show, for example, an increase in the consumption of Empire butter in the northern counties after a special campaign in 1931 and a displacement of foreign by Empire butter in Nottingham between 1928 and 1931.[146]

It was, of course, still difficult to interpret these factors, and not even the EMB claimed that such trends were solely due to the Board's propaganda. We know that the percentage of United Kingdom imports coming from the overseas Empire rose from thirty per cent of the total in 1926 to thirty seven per cent in 1933, but a substantial increase had already taken place before the Board was established, and the figure was to rise to thirty nine per cent in 1938 after the Board's demise.[147] The effect of advertising must in any case be set against the effect on consumption patterns firstly of the increasingly large and regular supplies of Empire products being offered customers alongside established European or American products and secondly the relative movements in prices between Empire and foreign prices which were in part a consequence. While a plausible case could be, and was, made out for the effectiveness of advertising, price factors may have been more important. The British Poster Advertising Association had reasonably claimed that the largest part of the mass market was too poor to be governed by much more than practical considerations relating to cost. Interestingly an EMB census of 1,000 grocers in 1928 disclosed that though there had been an overall increase in demand for Empire goods, this was recognised mainly by retailers in better class areas, where surplus income may be presumed to have existed, and was much less apparent in poorer districts, where the exigencies of price probably prevailed.[148] A sizeable portion of the population could not afford to have their pattern of consumption affected by ideological considerations. When the claims of the advertiser ran up against the contradictory knowledge and needs of the consumer, the limitations of publicity were exposed.

However, we know that the Publicity Committee and the Poster sub-committee interpreted their mission as also having long-term ideological and educational aims. It was for them not solely an immediate appeal to consumers, and they tuned the content of the posters and their distribution accordingly. It is therefore interesting to consider whether the EMB's publicity had more effect in propagating general imperial ideals among the public than in affecting their behaviour as consumers. We know that the EMB's publications and especially the posters effectively penetrated the educational system of the country, as the Board intended. It is a reflection of the prevailing imperial sentiment of the day that the propaganda dispatched to the schools was so uncritically received, blessed by the National Union of Teachers, endorsed by the Consultative Committee of the Board of Education, welcomed by the Annual Conference of Educational Associations. 'The Empire Marketing Board', wrote *London Teacher,* 'has made available for teachers...an enormous amount of valuable material....Most teachers agree that the EMB posters have been an excellent visual aid'. Late in 1929 the 22,000 schools currently being sent copies of EMB posters were asked if they wished to continue receiving them: ninety per cent did so. The Board collected many appreciative letters from teachers, and these reveal the way the EMB nurtured the Empire-centred nature of much inter-war teaching. 'The posters are of real value educationally and nationally, and quite fit in with my ideas of teaching geography, history and economics', wrote one recipient. 'These vivid posters will help us greatly to put before [the children] the idea of the British Empire as a great producing agent in the trade of mankind and in the service of the world as a whole', wrote another. 'Your posters have been a god-send to us', wrote a third, 'they vivify and intensify the very impression

we wish our pupils to receive with respect to the resources and potentialities of our Empire'. Gill's 'Highways of Empire' map was especially praised 'as a wonderful help both in Geography and History lessons'. Occasionally, the Board received letters of thanks apparently from the pupils, sometimes accompanied by little gifts such as a box of snowdrops from a country school in Yorkshire. According to at least one teacher the ideological purpose of the exercise was fulfilled: 'Your posters have created a new "Idea of Empire" in the minds of these poor little slum children here'.[149]

Of course, it is difficult to judge how effective this penetration really was, and where hard data is lacking, speculation must to an extent take over. It is at least difficult to disprove the contention that the EMB strengthened in the minds of the majority of school children a particular conception of Britain's status and power as the centre of a uniquely favoured imperial system. Moreover, the concepts of the Empire presented by the posters were apparently confirmed by other official and unofficial sources at the time and they dominated the educational system. Consequently these views of the world and Britain's place in it were scarcely challenged at this time by other less enthusiastic, more critical commentaries. Nor was there much in the personal experience of most people to enable them to judge independently the affairs of the wider world and the nature of the Empire. Accordingly the imperial messages written on the mind by EMB propagandists may indeed have been absorbed, if passively, because of the absence in this instance of contradictory data.

John Grierson was to claim in 1933 that the EMB's 'principal effect in six years has been to change the connotation of the word "Empire". Our command of peoples becomes solely a co-operative effort in the tilling of soil, the reaping of harvests and the organisation of a world economy. For the old flags of exploitation it substitutes the new flags of common labour'.[150] A similar claim was made by the art critic of *The Times* in March 1934. The occasion was elegiac, an exhibition of some 500 original poster designs prior to their sale, arranged for former EMB staff, admirers and the press. 'Until the Board began advertising', the critic claimed, 'the words "Empire" and "Imperial" were for all sensitive people fatally compromised'. Empire, he lamented, had been linked with too many distasteful, selfish, money-making schemes. But, thanks to the EMB's posters, 'Words and symbols which had become tainted by unfortunate associations were redeemed by art'.[151] On the one hand this comment was a tribute to the Empire Marketing Board. On the other it was a comment on the persuasive power of art. Art had been harnessed to a political purpose, and by this means the legitimacy of Empire had perhaps been revitalised for another generation.

FOOTNOTES

1   Letter from Sir Edward Parry, *The Times*, 24 Aug. 1933, p.6; leading article 30 Sept. 1933, p.11.

2   L.S. Amery, *My Political Life*, vol.2, Hutchinson, 1953, pp.354, 356: (place of publication London unless otherwise stated); Gervas Huxley, *Both Hands*, Chatto and Windus, 1970, pp.126-153; draft chapters of the unpublished account of the EMB written by its secretary Sir Stephen Tallents, Tallents Papers, Institute of Commonwealth Studies, Files 24-43.

3   Stephen Constantine, 'Bringing the Empire Alive: The Empire Marketing Board and imperial propaganda 1926-33' in John M. MacKenzie (ed.) *Imperialism and Popular Culture*, Manchester University Press, Manchester, 1986.

4   M. Ogilvy-Webb, *The Government Explains. A Study of the Information Services*, Allen and Unwin, 1965, pp.51-4; Sir Fife Clark, *The Central Office of Information*, Allen and Unwin, 1970, pp.22-34.

5   Michael Worboys, 'Science and British Colonial Imperialism 1895-1940', University of Oxford D.Phil. thesis 1979; Paul Swann, 'The British Documentary Film Movement, 1926-1946', University of Leeds Ph.D. thesis, 1979; Rachael Low, *The History of the British Film 1929-1939: Documentary and Educational Films of the 1930s*, Allen and Unwin, 1979, pp.51-64.

6   See also Judith Freeman, 'The Publicity of the Empire Marketing Board 1926-1933', *Journal of Advertising History*, vol.1, Dec. 1977, pp.12-14.

7   I.M. Drummond, *British Economic Policy and the Empire 1919-1939*, Allen and Unwin, 1972, pp.36-38; Stephen Constantine, *The Making of British Colonial Development Policy 1914-1940*, Cass, 1984, pp.9-194.

8   The detailed origins of the EMB may be traced in Baldwin Papers, Cambridge University Library, vol.XCIII 'Memo. on encouragement of Empire production' and covering letter by Cunliffe-Lister 5 Dec. 1924, vol.XXVII Churchill to Baldwin 6 Dec. 1924, vol.XCII Amery to Baldwin 28 Jan. 1926; Amery Papers, by permission of Mr. Julian Amery, Diary 1925 and 1926; PRO, Cabinet Memoranda, CAB 24/169/CP 543, CAB 24/175/CP 446, CP 458, CAB 24/178/CP 31, CP 54, CP 60, CAB 24/179/CP 112, CP 115; PRO Cabinet Conclusions, CAB 23/49/CAB 60(24)3, CAB 67(24)11, CAB 23/52/CAB 3(26)11, CAB 5(26)1, CAB 7(26)3, CAB 11(26)6; *Hansard*, Parliamentary Debates, House of Commons, vol.179, cols.1065-8; *Report of the Imperial Economic Committee*, Cmd.2493, 1925.

9   Tallents Papers, File 25, p.10.

10   Membership of the Board was printed as an appendix to the annual *Empire Marketing Board: Note on the Work and Finance of the Board*, Cmd.3158, 1928, Cmd.3372, 1929, Cmd.3637, 1930, Cmd.3914, 1931, Cmd.4121, 1932; *The Times*, 17 Nov. 1931, p.11.

11   The annual *Note on the Work and Finance of the EMB* gives details of the range of the Board's operations and the annual *Appropriations Accounts* in the Parliamentary Papers give figures for expenditure. Total EMB expenditure, including administrative and miscellaneous expenses, came to £3,702,884 in the eight financial years 1926-1933.

12   *Statistical Abstract for the British Empire 1925-1934*, Cmd.5016, 1935, pp.7-10.

13   *Report of the Imperial Economic Committee*, Cmd.2493, 1925, pp.6-10; *Hansard*, Parliamentary Debates, House of Commons vol.195, cols.887-967, 12 May 1926.

14   CAB 23/52/CAB 3(26)11, 3 Feb. 1926, quoting CP 458.

15   CAB 27/310 Cabinet Committee on Empire Marketing, EM(26)7 'Existing Arrangements for Government Advertising', note by Treasury, 18 Feb. 1926; Ogilvy-Webb, *The Government Explains*, pp.47-51; M.L. Sanders and P.M. Taylor, *British Propaganda During the First World War 1914-18*, Macmillan, 1977; Cate Haste, *Keep the Home Fires Burning: Propaganda in the First World War*, Allen Lane, 1977; P.M. Taylor, *The Projection of Britain*, Cambridge University Press, Cambridge, 1981.

16   PRO, CO 760/12, EMB minutes 2 June 1926.

17   T.R. Nevett, *Advertising in Britain*, Heinemann, 1982, pp.67-107, 141-159; E.S. Turner, *The Shocking History of Advertising*, Penguin, Harmondsworth, 1965, pp.132-138; W. Hamish Fraser, *The Coming of the Mass Market 1850-1914*, Macmillan, 1981, pp.134-46; H.F. Hutchinson, *The Poster. An Illustrated History from 1860*, Studio Vista, 1968, pp.9-102; B. Hillier, *Posters*, Hamlyn, 1969; Antony Griffiths, *Prints and Printmaking. An Introduction to the History and Techniques*, British Museum, 1980.

18   John M. MacKenzie, *Propaganda and Empire*, Manchester University Press, Manchester, 1984, pp.23-30; Michael J. Winstanley, *The Shopkeeper's World 1830-1914*, Manchester University Press, Manchester 1983, pp.78-9; Robert Opie, *Rule Britannia. Trading on the British Image*, Viking, Harmondsworth, 1985, pp.14-20; *Durham County Advertiser*, 1 Jan. 1932, p.12.

19   G.H. Saxon Mills, *There is a Tide...: The Life and Work of Sir William Crawford*, Heinemann, 1927, p.129. *The Times*, 28 June 1927, p.9.

20   Christian Barman, *The Man Who Built London Transport*, David and Charles, Newton Abbot, 1979; Turner, *The Shocking History of Advertising*, p.245. For membership of the EMB's committees see appendices to the annual published reports *Empire Marketing Board*, EMB 9, 19, 28, 41, 53 and 63.

21   No biography of Tallents has yet been written but see *Who Was Who* (died 1958); Amery, *My Political Life*, vol.II, p.347; Huxley, *Both Hands*, pp.128-9; *The Times*, 13 Sept. 1958, p.11; and Sir Stephen Tallents, 'Salesmanship in the public service', *Public Administration*, vol.II, 1933, pp.259-66. He was knighted in 1932.

22   Total expenditure on the press campaign £364,280, on exhibitions and shopping weeks £277,771, on cinema £76,512, on lectures £35,320 and on miscellaneous activities £43,699. For details see

Constantine, 'Bringing the Empire Alive' and the annual *Note on the Work and Finance of the Empire Marketing Board*.

23 CO 760/23, Publicity Committee minutes 8 July 1926.

24 Technically this was the Poster Section of the First Sub-Committee (which dealt also with press advertisements) of the Publicity Committee and is so described on the bound volume of its minutes and papers in the Public Record Office, CO 760/26. But the Section always referred to itself as a sub-committee and this nomenclature has been adopted in the text.

25 Amery, *My Political Life*, pp.347, 352; Huxley, *Both Hands*, p.127; Tallents Papers, File 33, p.2.

26 CO 956/734. References to CO 956 are to the EMB Poster Collection in the PRO. Sizes given in the text are by width then height.

27 A portion is preserved as CO 956/462B. A third, unused, original design also by Herrick is kept in the Victoria and Albert Museum.

28 Also by F.C. Harrison, Horace Taylor and Tom Purvis: CO 956/463-71.

29 CO 956/551-601.

30 CO 956/602-55.

31 CO 956/656-81.

32 CO 760/26 Poster section minutes 13 April and 4 Aug. 1927.

33 CO 956/344-75; CO 760/23 Publicity Committee minutes 25 Sept. 1928; CO 760/26 Poster section minutes 16 May 1929.

34 CO 956/320-31.

35 Of which 89 complete or partial sets are in CO 956 in the PRO and part or all of 15 sets are in the Victoria and Albert Museum (including some original designs).

36 Quotations from Sir William Crawford 'The Artist in Advertising: Stating the Problem', *Commercial Art*, vol.5, 1928, p.146 and Tallents Papers File 25, p.4. See also CO 760/22/EMB/P.C./2 'Notes on a Scheme of Poster Display'.

37 Sir William Crawford, 'The Poster Campaign of the Empire Marketing Board', *Commercial Art*, vol.6, 1929, p.131 and 'Making the Empire "Come Alive", *ibid.* vol.1, 1926, p.241.

38 CO 760/26 Poster section minutes 4 Nov. 1926, 2 June 1927, 14 March 1929.

39 *Ibid.* 20 Dec. 1928; see also 7 May 1931.

40 *Ibid.*; it is not clear from the minutes 12 March 1931 whether Sutherland had actually submitted designs himself in search of a commission.

41 *Ibid.* 1 Dec. 1926, 14 March, 3 Oct. and 7 Nov. 1929, 10 July 1930.

42. *Ibid.* 1 Dec. 1926, 17 Feb. and 3 March 1927, 3 Feb. 1928.

43 *Ibid.* 6 Jan. 1927, 13 Sept. 1928, 28 Aug. 1930; some sketches appear to have been obtained from Whistler 9 Oct. 1930.

44 *Ibid.* 19 Nov. 1926, 12 May, 16 June and 27 Oct. 1927. Hassall's 'Skegness is *so* Bracing' poster of 1909 has been much reproduced, see for example Hillier, *Posters*, p.87.

45 M. Haworth-Booth, *E. McKnight Kauffer: A Designer and his Public*, Gordon Fraser, 1979.

46 CO 760/26 Poster section minutes 11 April 1929, 28 Aug. 1930.

47 *Ibid.* 29 Aug. 1929, CO 956/217-22.

48 CO 760/26 Poster section minutes 12 May, 16 June, 4 Aug. and 15 Dec. 1927, 12 Jan., 8 March, 12 April, 24 May and 4 Oct. 1928; CO 760/23 Publicity Committee minutes 27 March 1929. Suddaby's Liner set is, alas, missing from the collection.

49 CO 760/26 Poster section minutes 14 June 1928.

50 *Ibid.* 10 Nov. 1927 and 3 Feb. 1928 and CO 956/199-204, 491-8.

51 CO 760/26 Poster section minutes 23 April and 7 May 1931, 21 Nov. and 19 Dec. 1929.

52 CO 760/23 Publicity Committee minutes 16 July 1926; CO 760/26 Poster section minutes 7 Feb. 1929.

53 *Ibid.* 1 Dec. 1926, 13 April 1927, 6 Jan. 1927.

54 *Ibid.* 18 April, 9 May and 12 Sept. 1929, 10 July 1930.

55 *Ibid.* 14 June and 30 Aug. 1928.

56 *Ibid.* 5 July and 21 June 1928.

57 *Ibid.* 29 May 1930.

58 *Ibid.* 30 May, 13 June, 29 Aug., 5 Sept. 1929.

59 Our knowledge of the production of this map is enriched by the EMB file CO 758/60/5 generated by Lt. Col. S. Smith who accused the Board of breaching his copyright to the projection. See also Tallents Papers File 33, p.3.

60 CO 760/26 Poster section minutes 3 Feb. 1928, 1 Dec. 1926.

61 *Ibid.* 8 and 29 May 1930.

62 *Ibid.* 4 and 11 Nov. 1926.

63 *Ibid.* 11 and 19 Nov. and 1 Dec. 1926, 6 Jan. and 10 Feb. 1927; 13 April and 31 Aug. 1927, 12 Jan. and 31 May 1928.

64 *Ibid.* 16 March 1928.

65 *Ibid.* 4 Aug. 1922, 5 Sept., 3 Oct. and 5 Dec. 1929, 23 Jan. and 10 July 1930.

66 *Ibid.* 29 March 1928, 18 April 1929.

67 Receiving 52 guineas for their trouble. *Ibid.* 30 May, 27 June, 25 July, 21 Nov. and 19 Dec. 1929, 2 and 23 Jan. 1930.

68 *Ibid.* 4 and 11 Nov. and 1 Dec. 1926: 100 copies of the first design were pulled for the record and one signed print survives in the PRO CO 956/721.

69 CO 760/26 Poster section minutes 3 Feb., 10 May, 21 June, 5 July, 4 Oct. and 15 Nov. 1928.

70 Tallents Papers, File 33, p.2.

71 CO 760/26 Poster section minutes 2, 9 and 30 May, 20 June, 29 Aug., 5 and 19 Sept. and 7 Nov. 1929. The designs were later sold and separated and the complete series reassembled for display for the first time since the 1940s at the Royal Academy Stanley Spencer Exhibition in 1980. The catalogue reproduces and comments on the pictures, pp.114-8. The episode is also mentioned in Haworth-Booth, *McKnight Kauffer*, p.47.

72 CO 760/26 Poster section minutes 29 Sept. 1927, 12 Jan. 1928, 30 May 1929.

73 *Ibid.* 10 Feb., 29 Sept. and 13 Oct. 1927, 10 May 1928, 7 May 1931.

74 *Ibid.* 31 May 1928, 11 June 1931; CO 758/107/5.

75 CO 760/26 Poster section minutes 19 Nov. 1926, 10 July 1930, 6 Jan. and 10 Feb. 1927.

76 *Ibid.* 6. 13 and 27 June 1929.

77 *Ibid.* 6 Jan., 2 June, 15 Dec. 1927.

78 *Ibid.* 27 Oct. 1926, 3 Feb. 1927.

79 *Ibid.* 28 May 1931.

80 *Ibid.* 4, 18 and 31 Aug. 1927.

81 *Ibid.* 11 Nov. 1926, 6 Jan. and 3 March 1927. He was more successful in negotiations over his large hoarding poster, *ibid.* 12 May and 18 Aug. 1927.

82 *Ibid.* 30 May and 7 Nov. 1929.

83 *Ibid.* 27 Oct. and 9 Dec. 1926, 13 June 1929, 27 Feb., 29 May and 10 July 1930.

84 *Ibid.* 19 Nov. 1926.

85 *Ibid.* 14 June 1928. These animal designs by F.C. Herrick were subsequently reprinted as posters, using another company (Plate 43).

86 CO 758/103/7 Russell Palmer to Huxley 9 Dec. 1928.

87 CO 760/26 Poster section minutes 3 March 1927. See also Anthony Bertram, *Paul Nash,* Faber, 1955, p.189.

88 CO 760/26 Poster section minutes 23 Oct. 1930, 9 April 1931. The original designs are now in the V and A. See also John Woodeson, *Mark Gertler,* Sidgwick and Jackson, 1972, p.384.

89 CO 956/49; information from his daughter and record by Tallents in family papers.

90 CO 760/26 Poster section minutes 3 and 18 March, 18 Aug., 29 Sept. 1927; CO 758/103/8 and 9 especially Huxley to Pick 13 Dec. 1928.

91 CO 758/103/7 Vincent Brooks Day to Pick 21 Jan. 1927.

92 CO 758/103/9 Huxley to Pick 13 Dec. 1928.

93 CO 760/26 Poster section minutes 11 Nov. 1926, 21 Nov. 1929, 23 Jan. and 3 April 1930. The new type design prepared by Gill was called 'Solus': it is described and illustrated in Roy Brewer, *Eric Gill. The Man Who Loved Letters,* Muller, 1973, pp.70-1.

94 T.E. Griffits, *The Technique of Colour Printing by Lithography,* Faber, 1940, p.20.

95 CO 758/103/7, statement by HMSO.

96 CO 760/23 Publicity Committee minutes, 3 Aug. and 1 Dec. 1926; CO 760/26 Poster section minutes 3 March 1927.

97 CO 760/23 Publicity Committee minutes 25 Sept. 1928; Tallents Papers, File 33, p.9.

98   CO 760/23 Publicity Committee minutes 12 Dec. 1928, 27 March 1929 and CO 760/22/PC/117 Publicity Committee papers, Progress Report 20 Sept. 1929.
99   CO 760/23 Publicity Committee minutes 3 Aug. and 7 Oct. 1926, 5 Dec. 1927; CO 760/26 Poster section minutes 1 Dec. 1926; CO 758/103/7 Pick to Tallents 10 Jan. 1927; Tallents Papers File 33, p.8.
100   *Note on the Work and Finance of the Board*, Cmd.4121, p.16; Tallents Papers Files 6 and 14; CO 956/338-43, 376-81.
101   CO 760/26 Poster section minutes 4 Aug. 1927.
102   *Ibid.* 9 Feb. and 4 Oct. 1928, 21 Nov. 1929.
103   *Ibid.* 9 and 16 May and 13 June 1929; 3 Feb. and 10 May 1928.
104   *Ibid.* 5 and 19 Dec. 1929; CO 760/23 Publicity Committee minutes 23 Jan. 1929.
105   *Ibid.* 16 July 1929; see Constantine, 'Bringing the Empire Alive', pp.212-4.
106   CO 760/26 Poster section minutes 11 Nov. 1926.
107   CO 760/23 Publicity Committee minutes 24 Feb. 1927; CO 760/22/PC/29 1 March 1927.
108   Distinguished by the prefix R before the EMB poster reference number: see the copies in CO 956/515-45.
109   *Empire Marketing Board*, EMB 28 and EMB 41.
110   CO 760/26 Poster section minutes 31 Aug. 1927.
111   *The Times* 1 Sept. 1927 p.11; CO 760/23 Publicity Committee minutes 15 Sept. 1927; *Note on the work and Finance of the Board*, Cmd.2898, 1927, p.10; *Empire Marketing Board*, EMB 9, p.38, EMB 632, p.103.
112   *Macmillan's Class Pictures: Reference Book, History, Geography and Literature*, Macmillan, 1932.
113   CO 760/23 Publicity Committee minutes 7 April and 9 June 1927, 12 Nov. 1930, 15 Jan. 1931; CO 760/26 Poster section minutes 30 June 1927; CO 760/22/PC/36 6 April 1927; CO 760/12 EMB minutes 26 Nov. 1930.
114   CO 760/26 Poster section minutes, 29 May, 28 Aug. and 23 Oct. 1930; CO 760/23 Publicity Committee minutes 12 Nov. 1930; the posters are CO 956/229-34.
115   Sir Stephen Tallents, 'The Empire Marketing Board 1926-1933', *United Empire*, vol.XXIV, 1933, p.484; CO 760/12 EMB minutes 2 June 1926; Sir William Crawford, 'Making the Empire "Come Alive",' *Commercial Art*, vol.1, 1926, p.241 and 'The Poster Campaign of the Empire Marketing Board', *ibid.*, vol.6, 1929, p.131.
116   And see CO 956/115, 151, 153, 155, 463, 552, 582, 600, 603, 606A.
117   CO 956/236, 237, 418-22, 510.
118   CO 956/378.
119   CO 956/695
120   CO 956/62-7, 443, 486, 713, 718, 719. For an account of the ceremonial public mixing of the first King's Empire Christmas Pudding read and relish the reports in *The Times* 20 Dec. 1926, p.9, 21 Dec. 1926 p.9, photo. p.16, 23 Dec. 1926, p.12.
121   CO 956/14-16, 37, 546-550B.

122   CO 956/133-8, 145-9, 175-80, 181-86, 187-92, 217-22, 258-63.
123   CO 956/344-75 and see similarly contract labels CO 956/320-31.
124   CO 956/238, 338.
125   CO 956/107-11, 211-16.
126   CO 956/1, 2, 77, 106, 381, 409-13, 425, 427, 481.
127   CO 956/482.
128   CO 956/481-3, 529-30, 223-28.
129   CO 956/59, 113, 235-9, 332-6, 397-401, 435, 437, 445-9: most of these feature flags and are the work of Austin Cooper.
130   A set featuring the Empire tour of the Duke and Duchess of York appears to be lost; CO 760/22/PC 42 7 June 1927.
131   CO 760/22/PC/11 30 Aug. 1926. Compare the images discussed in J.O. Springhall, '"Up Guards and At Them": British Imperialism and Popular Art', in MacKenzie (ed.) *Imperialism and Popular Culture*, pp.49-72.
132   Tallents Papers File 25 pp.5-6, File 32 p.32; Sir Stephen Tallents, 'The Communication of Ideas', *International Year Book and Statesmen's Who's Who*, 1957, p.2; Sanders and Taylor, *British Propaganda in the First World War*, pp.248-50, 264.
133   Marion Yass, *This is Your War; Home Front Propaganda in the Second World War*, HMSO, 1983, pp.5, 19; Ian McLaine, *Ministry of Morale*, Allen & Unwin, pp.13-14; Ogilvy-Webb, *The Government Explains*; Clark, *The Central Office of Information*.
134   J. Barnes and D. Nicholson (eds.), *The Leo Amery Diaries*, vol.1, Hutchinson, 1980, 20 July 1927; Neville Chamberlain Papers, by permission of the Head of Special Collections University of Birmingham Library, NC 2/22 Diary 21 July 1927; Baldwin Papers vol.IV, Amery to Baldwin, 19 July 1927; CAB 23/55/CAB 41(27)7, CAB 42(27)6.
135   Annual *Reports from the Select Committee of Public Accounts*, 1926-7 to 1932-3; *Reports from the Select Committee on Estimates*, 1928 and 1932; *Report of the Committee on National Expenditure*, Cmd.3920, 1931, pp.131-2; Annual *Appropriation Accounts*.
136   CO 760/22/PC 155, 163, 171, 184, 185, 217; CO 760/12 EMB minutes 12 Feb., 14 May and 30 July 1930 and 21 Jan. and 1 Dec. 1931.
137   CO 760/23 Publicity Committee minutes 14 Dec. 1931; Huxley, *Both Hands*, p.153.
138   *Note on the Work and Finance of the E.M.B.*, Cmd.4121, 1932, p.9; Nevett, *Advertising in Britain*, p.146.
139   CO 956/403-8.
140   *Imperial Conference at Ottawa 1932 Summary of Proceedings*, Cmd.4174, 1932, p.14; *Report of the Imperial Committee on Economic Consultation and Co-operation*, Cmd.4335, 1933, pp.48-92.
141   CO 760/26 Poster section minutes 16 June 1927; *The Times*, 3 Nov. 1926, p.11; CO 758/104/1; *Advertising World*, vol.52, 1927, p.844.

142   *Commercial Art*, vol.3, Sept. 1927; vol.4, Feb. 1928; vol.13, July 1932; vol.15, Aug. 1933; CO 760/12 EMB minutes 8 Dec. 1926; *The Times* 3 Nov. 1926, p.11; CO 758/104/2; CO 760/26 Poster section minutes 21 Nov. 1929.
143   CO 760/22/PC 126; CO 760/26 Poster section minutes 5 Dec. 1929; CO 760/23 Publicity Committee minutes 12 Dec. 1929 and 9 June 1927.
144   *Select Committee on Estimates*, 1928, question 1287; CO 760/12 EMB minutes 1 May 1979; CO 760/7/696; Tallents Papers Files 5, 7 and 12; CO 769/22/PC 93; CO 760/23 Publicity Committee minutes 12 Dec. 1928; CO 758/104/2.
145   See EMB reports nos. 19, 28, 41, 53, 63.
146   CO 760/7/655; *Changes in the Demand for Butter*, EMB 39, 1931; *Further Changes in the Demand for Butter*, EMB 48, 1932; *Select Committee on Estimates*, 1932, question 304. Other EMB reports dealt with the demand for cheese in London, canned fruits, honey, canned vegetables, and South African fruits.
147   *Statistical Abstract for the British Empire 1925-34*, Cmd.5016, 1935, pp.3-4; Drummond, *British Economic Policy and the Empire*, pp.20-1.
148   *Select Committee on Estimates*, 1928, p.xvii, question 1651.
149   CO 760/22/PC 29, 93, 130, 192; CO 760/23 Publicity Committee minutes 23 Jan. and 27 March 1929; CO 760/5/EMB 482; Tallents Papers Files 7 and 14.
150   John Grierson, 'The EMB Film Unit', *Cinema Quarterly*, Summer 1933, p.204.
151   CO 758/99/5; *The Times*, 20 March 1934, p.11.

THE PLATES

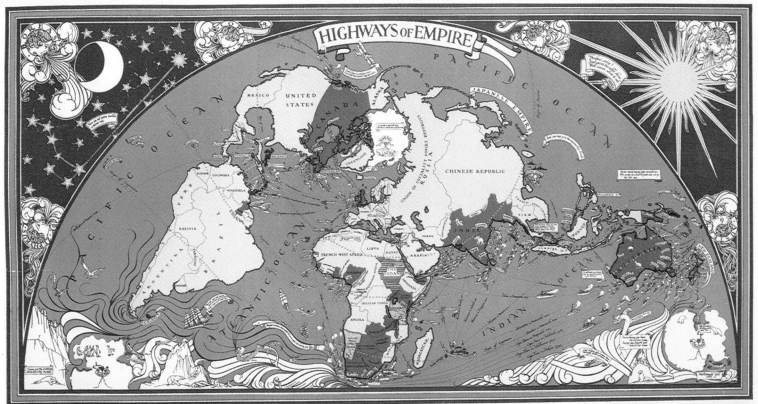

PLATE 1
Artist: MacDonald Gill
Title: Highways of Empire
Displayed: as a hoarding poster January 1927
Printer: Jordison and Co. Ltd., London and Middlesbrough
Size: 30 ins.×20 ins.
EMB ref: RSWBO (reprint for schools and public purchase)
PRO ref: CO 956/537A

PLATE 2A
Artist: R.P. Gossop
Title: Australia Sends to Us   We Send to Australia
Top Caption: Empire Buying Brings Prosperity
Displayed: May 1927
Printer: John Waddington and Co. Ltd., Leeds and London
Sizes: 60 ins. × 40 ins. and 25 ins. × 40 ins.
EMB ref: E1-E5
PRO ref: CO 956/457-461

PLATE 2B
Artist: Pat Keely
Top Caption: Speed Empire Trade
Displayed: February-March 1931
Printer: John Horn Ltd., London and Glasgow
Sizes: 60 ins. × 40 ins. and 25 ins. × 40 ins.
EMB ref: BY1-BY5
PRO ref: CO 956/247-251

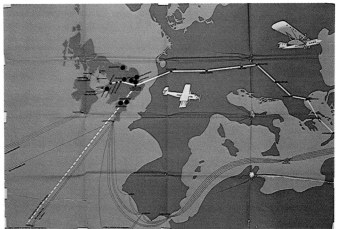 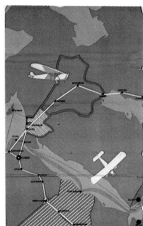

"To seek such things as we lacke, as also to carry unto them such things as they lacke, so that hereby not only commoditie may ensue both to them and us, but also an indissoluble and perpetual league of friendship."

Letter to Sir Hugh Willoughby 1553

WE SEND TO AUSTRALIA

Galvanized Iron Goods	2,135,000	Cotton Piece goods	8,090,000	Cranes, etc.	180,000	Motor Cars & Chassis	2,310,000	Printing Paper	2,640,000
Tin Plate	1,170,000	Made-up goods	740,000	Agricultural Machinery	230,000	Motor Cycles		Writing Paper	230,000
Wire, etc.	610,000	Thread	440,000	Prime Movers	430,000		380,000	Other Paper	500,000
Welded Tubes	700,000	Lace & Net	140,000	Electrical Machinery	1,000,000	Tractors	190,000		
Bars, Rods, etc.	750,000	Cotton Yarns	500,000	Other Machinery	2,350,000	Accessories & Parts	290,000		
Other Iron Goods	2,500,000	Other Cotton Goods	540,000						

1925 Total Trade £60,170,000

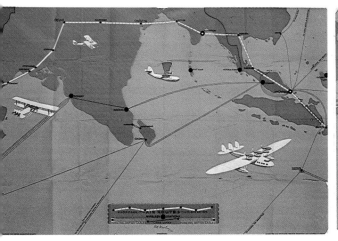

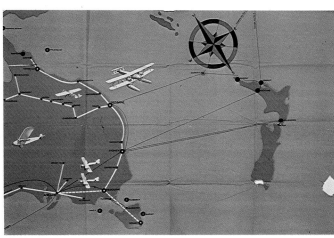

PLATE 3A
Artist: J. Kerr Lawson
Title: They Shall Beat Their Swords Into Plowshares...
Top Caption: The Empire Stands for Peace
Displayed: November 1929
Printer: Eyre and Spottiswoode Ltd., London
Sizes: 60 ins. × 40 ins. and 25 ins. × 40 ins.
EMB ref: BB1-BB5
PRO ref: CO 956/127-131

PLATE 3B
Artist: J. Kerr Lawson
Title: The People Bring Much More Than Enough...
Top Caption: Service of Empire
Displayed: November 1932
Printer: St Michael's Press Ltd., West Norwood, London
Sizes: 60 ins. × 40 ins. and 25 ins. × 40 ins.
EMB ref: CG1-CG5
PRO ref: CO 956/296-300

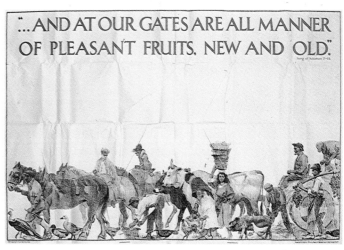

PLATE 4
Artist: F.C. Herrick
Title: New Zealand Dairy
Top Caption:
Come up, come in from Eastward, from the guard-
ports of the morn,
Beat up, beat in from southerly, O Gipsies of the
Horn,
Swift shuttles of an Empire's loom that weaves us,
main to main,
The coastwise lights of England give you welcome
back again!
Rudyard Kipling

Displayed: January-February 1927
Printer: Vincent Brooks Day and Son Ltd., London
Size: 60 ins. × 40 ins.
EMB ref: A5
PRO ref: CO 956/3

PLATE 5
Artist: E.A. Cox
Title: Sugar Growing in Mauritius
Displayed: March 1927
Printer: Eyre and Spottiswoode Ltd., London
Size: 60 ins. × 40 ins.
EMB ref: B1
PRO ref: CO 956/116

PLATE 6
Artist: Charles Pears
Title: Suez Canal
Displayed: March 1927
Printer: Waterlow and Sons Ltd., London
Size: 60 ins. × 40 ins.
EMB ref: B3
PRO ref: CO 956/118

MOTOR MANUFACTURING

PLATE 7
Artist: Clive Gardiner
Title: Motor Manufacturing
Top Caption: Empire Buying Makes Busy
Factories
Displayed: September 1928
Printer: Waterlow and Sons Ltd., London
Size: 60 ins. × 40 ins.
EMB ref: C1
PRO ref: CO 956/258

A BLAST FURNACE

PLATE 8
Artist: Clive Gardiner
Title: A Blast Furnace
Top Caption: Empire Buying Makes Busy
Factories
Displayed: September 1928
Printer: Waterlow and Sons Ltd., London
Size: 60 ins. × 40 ins.
EMB ref: C3
PRO ref: CO 956/260

MAKING ELECTRICAL MACHINERY

PLATE 9
Artist: Clive Gardiner
Title: Making Electrical Machinery
Top Caption: Empire Buying Makes Busy
Factories
Displayed: September 1928
Printer: Waterlow and Sons Ltd., London
Size: 60 ins. × 40 ins.
EMB ref: C5
PRO ref: CO 956/262

PLATE 10
Artist: G. Spencer Pryse
Title: A Rice Field in India
Displayed: April 1927
Printer: Vincent Brooks Day and Son Ltd., London
Size: 60 ins. × 40 ins.
EMB ref: D1
PRO ref: CO 956/424

PLATE 11
Artist: Fred Taylor
Title: The Empire Shop
Displayed: April 1927
Printer: Waterlow and Sons Ltd.
Size: 60 ins. × 40 ins.
EMB ref: D3
PRO ref: CO 956/426

PLATE 12
Artist: G. Spencer Pryse
Title: Tea Picking in Ceylon
Displayed: April 1927
Printer: Vincent Brooks Day and Son Ltd., London
Size: 60 ins. × 40 ins.
EMB ref: D5
PRO ref: CO 956/722

K5. ISSUED BY THE EMPIRE MARKETING BOARD   CATTLE RAISING - AUSTRALIA   PRINTED FOR H.M.STATIONERY OFFICE BY HAYCOCK, CADLE & GRAHAM, LTD. LONDON. S.E.5.

PLATE 13
Artist: Gregory Brown
Title: Cattle Raising - Australia
Displayed: November 1927
Printer: Haycock, Cadle and Graham Ltd., London
Size: 60 ins. × 40 ins.
EMB ref: K5
PRO ref: CO 956/480

Empire Builders.

PLATE 14
Artist: Fred Taylor
Title: Empire Builders
Top Caption: Today Trade Builds the Empire
Displayed: October-November 1927
Printer: Thomas Forman and Sons, Nottingham
Size: 30 ins. × 20 ins. (reprint for schools and public purchase)
EMB ref: RL3
PRO ref: CO 956/529

A SUDAN COTTON FIELD

M.1 ISSUED BY THE EMPIRE MARKETING BOARD

Printed For H.M. STATIONERY OFFICE by JOHNSON RIDDLE & Cº Lᵀᴰ LONDON. S.E.I.

PLATE 15
Artist: E. Barnard Lintott
Title: A Sudan Cotton Field
Top Caption: Empire Trade is Growing
Displayed: December 1927-January 1928
Printer: Johnson, Riddle and Co. Ltd., London
Size: 60 ins. × 40 ins.
EMB ref: M1
PRO ref: CO 956/484

PLATE 16
Artist: E. McKnight Kauffer
Title: Cocoa
Top Caption: One Third of the Empire is in the
Tropics
Displayed: September–October 1927
Printer: Haycock, Cadle and Graham Ltd., London
Size: 60 ins. × 40 ins.
EMB ref: N1
PRO ref: CO 956/499

PLATE 17
Artist: E. McKnight Kauffer
Title: Jungles Today are Gold Mines To-Morrow
Top Caption: One Third of the Empire is in the
Tropics
Displayed: September–October 1927
Printer: Haycock, Cadle and Graham Ltd., London
Size: 60 ins. × 40 ins.
EMB ref: N3
PRO ref: CO 956/501

BANANA PALMS

PLATE 18
Artist: E. McKnight Kauffer
Title: *Banana Palms*
Top Caption: One Third of the Empire is in the
Tropics
Displayed: September–October 1927
Printer: Haycock, Cadle and Graham Ltd., London
Size: 60 ins. × 40 ins.
EMB ref: N5
PRO ref: CO 956/503

THE RIVER MERSEY

PLATE 19
Artist: Charles Dixon
Title: The River Mersey
Top Caption: The Western Gateway of Empire
Displayed: September–October (?) 1928
Printer: John Waddington and Co. Ltd., Leeds and London
Size: 60 ins. × 40 ins.
EMB ref: O3
PRO ref: CO 956/506

PLATE 20
Artist: Austin Cooper
Title: From Christmas to Christmas May Empire
Trade Increase
Top Caption: A Happy New Year to the Empire
Displayed: December 1927
Printer: Waterlow and Sons Ltd., London
Size: 60 ins. × 40 ins.
EMB ref: R3
PRO ref: CO 956/511

PLATE 21
Artist: H.S. Williamson
Top Caption: John Bull, Sons and Daughters
Displayed: January-February 1928
Printer: Eyre and Spottiswoode Ltd., London
Size: 60 ins. × 40 ins.
EMB ref: T3
PRO ref: CO 956/684

PLATE 22
Artist: Charles Pears
Title: Gibraltar
Top Caption: The Empire's Highway to India
Displayed: May 1928
Printer: Johnson, Riddle and Co. Ltd., London
Size: 60 ins. × 40 ins.
EMB ref: U1
PRO ref: CO 956/688

MALTA

IN 1927 THE IMPORTS OF INDIAN GOODS INTO THE UNITED KINGDOM AMOUNTED TO £66,000,000.
INDIA IS THE WORLD'S BIGGEST CUSTOMER FOR BRITISH GOODS.

U2 ISSUED BY THE EMPIRE MARKETING BOARD   PRINTED FOR H.M STATIONERY OFFICE BY JOHNSON RIDDLE & CO LTD LONDON S.E.1

PLATE 23
Artist: Charles Pears
Title: Malta
Top Caption: The Empire's Highway to India
Displayed: May 1928
Printer: Johnson, Riddle and Co. Ltd., London
Size: 25 ins. × 40 ins.
EMB ref: U2
PRO ref: CO 956/689

PLATE 24
Artist: Charles Pears
Title: Suez Canal
Top Caption: The Empire's Highway to India
Displayed: May 1928
Printer: Johnson, Riddle and Co. Ltd., London
Size: 25 ins. × 40 ins.
EMB ref: U3
PRO ref: CO 956/690

ADEN

IN 1927 THE EXPORT OF UNITED KINGDOM PRODUCTS TO INDIA AMOUNTED TO £86,000,000. ••• SUPPORT YOUR OWN BEST CUSTOMER BY ASKING ALWAYS FOR EMPIRE GOODS.

U4 ISSUED BY THE EMPIRE MARKETING BOARD   PRINTED FOR H.M STATIONERY OFFICE BY JOHNSON RIDDLE & CO LTD LONDON, S.E.I

PLATE 25
Artist: Charles Pears
Title: Aden
Top Caption: The Empire's Highway to India
Displayed: May 1928
Printer: Johnson, Riddle and Co. Ltd., London
Size: 25 ins. × 40 ins.
EMB ref: U4
PRO ref: CO 956/691

PLATE 26
Artist: Charles Pears
Title: Bombay
Top Caption: The Empire's Highway to India
Displayed: May 1928
Printer: Johnson, Riddle and Co. Ltd., London
Size: 60 ins. × 40 ins.
EMB ref: U5
PRO ref: CO 956/692

V.1. ISSUED BY THE EMPIRE MARKETING BOARD.   A PADDY FIELD   PRINTED FOR H.M. STATIONERY OFFICE BY EYRE & SPOTTISWOODE LTD H.M. PRINTERS, LONDON.

BA NYAN

PLATE 27
Artist: Ba Nyan
Title: A Paddy Field
Top Caption: Burmah   A Land of Rich Resources
Displayed: February 1928
Printer: Eyre and Spottiswoode Ltd., London
Size: 60 ins. × 40 ins.
EMB ref: V1
PRO ref: CO 956/694

BA NYAN.

TIMBER STACKING

V.3. ISSUED BY THE EMPIRE MARKETING BOARD.   PRINTED FOR H. M. STATIONERY OFFICE BY EYRE & SPOTTISWOODE LTD H. M. PRINTERS. LONDON.

PLATE 28
Artist: Ba Nyan
Title: *Timber Stacking*
Top Caption: Burmah   A Land of Rich Resources
Displayed: February 1928
Printer: Eyre and Spottiswoode Ltd., London
Size: 60 ins. × 40 ins.
EMB ref: V3
PRO ref: CO 956/696

GATHERING COCOA PODS

AA1 ISSUED BY THE EMPIRE MARKETING BOARD. (LITHOGRAPH BY SPENCER PRYSE.)   PRINTED FOR H.M. STATIONERY OFFICE BY NATHANIEL LLOYD & CO. LTD. LONDON, S.E. 1.

PLATE 29
Artist: G. Spencer Pryse
Title: Gathering Cocoa Pods
Top Caption: What Gold Coast Prosperity Means
Displayed: April 1928
Printer: Nathaniel Lloyd and Co. Ltd., London
Size: 60 ins. × 40 ins.
EMB ref: AA1
PRO ref: CO 956/5

SORTING MANGANESE ORE

PLATE 30
Artist: G. Spencer Pryse
Title: Sorting Manganese Ore
Top Caption: What Gold Coast Prosperity Means
Displayed: April 1928
Printer: Nathaniel Lloyd and Co. Ltd., London
Size: 60 ins. × 40 ins.
EMB ref: AA5
PRO ref: CO 956/8

COLOMBO. CEYLON

PLATE 31
Artist: Kenneth D. Shoesmith
Title: Colombo Ceylon
Top Caption: Our Trade with the East
Displayed: December 1928
Printer: Waterlow and Sons Ltd., London
Size: 60 ins. × 40 ins.
EMB ref: AD1
PRO ref: CO 956/13

PLATE 32
Artist: John Nash
Title: Fruit Gardens and Orchard
Top Caption: Home Gardens for Home Markets
Displayed: June 1930
Printer: Eyre and Spottiswoode Ltd., London
Size: 60 ins. × 40 ins.
EMB ref: AG5
PRO ref: CO 956/63

PLATE 33
Artist: John Keating
Title: Irish Free State Pigs
Displayed: June–July 1929
Printer: Waterlow and Sons Ltd., London,
Dunstable, Watford
Size: 60 ins. × 40 ins.
EMB ref: AH5
PRO ref: CO 956/38

SOUTH AFRICAN ORANGE ORCHARDS

PLATE 34
Artist: Guy Kortright
Title: South African Orange Orchards
Top Caption: Summer's Oranges from South Africa
Displayed: August 1928
Printer: Waterlow and Sons Ltd., London,
Dunstable, Watford
Size: 60 ins. × 40 ins.
EMB ref: AJ3
PRO ref: CO 956/41

A.M.1. Issued by the Empire Marketing Board

AUSTRALIAN WHEAT

Printed for H.M. Stationery Office by Chorley & Pickersgill Ltd. Printers. Leeds and London

PLATE 35
Artist: A.M. Webb
Title: Australian Wheat
Top Caption: Australia's Wealth of Wheat and Wool
Displayed: January 1929
Printer: Chorley and Pickersgill Ltd., Leeds and London
Size: 60 ins. × 40 ins.
EMB ref: AM1
PRO ref: CO 956/51

PLATE 36
Artist: F.C. Harrison
Title: Making the Empire Christmas Pudding
Top Caption: Christmas Fare from the Empire
Displayed: November–December 1928
Printer: Eyre and Spottiswoode Ltd., London
Size: 60 ins. × 40 ins.
EMB ref: AO1
PRO ref: CO 956/62

PLATE 37
Artist: Clare Leighton
Title: Sheep
Top Caption: Help Home Farms Buy British
Displayed: August 1929
Printer: Waterlow and Sons Ltd., London
Size: 60 ins. × 40 ins.
EMB ref: AP1
PRO ref: CO 956/68

A.S.1. ISSUED BY THE EMPIRE MARKETING BOARD.   PRINTED FOR H.M. STATIONERY OFFICE BY WATERLOW & SONS LTD. LONDON, DUNSTABLE & WATFORD.

PLATE 38
Artist: A.A. Moore
Title: Isles of Scilly
Top Caption: Home Bulbs for Home Gardens
Displayed: March-April 1929
Printer: Waterlow and Sons Ltd., London
Size: 60 ins. × 40 ins.
EMB ref: AS1
PRO ref: CO 956/84

Tobacco Plantation in S. RHODESIA

PLATE 39
Artist: Frank E. Pape
Title: Tobacco Plantation in Southern Rhodesia
Top Caption: Smoke Empire Tobacco
Displayed: June 1929
Printer: Johnson, Riddle and Co. Ltd., London
Size: 60 ins. × 40 ins.
EMB ref: AU1
PRO ref: CO 956/90

SMOKE · EMPIRE · TOBACCO

PLATE 40
Artist: Frank E. Pape
Title: Smoke Empire Tobacco
Top Caption: Smoke Empire Tobacco
Displayed: June 1929
Printer: Johnson, Riddle and Co. Ltd., London
Size: 60 ins. × 40 ins.
EMB ref: AU3
PRO ref: CO 956/92

Tobacco Plantation in NYASALAND

Printed For H.M. STATIONERY OFFICE by JOHNSON RIDDLE & Cº LTº LONDON. S.E.1.

PLATE 41
Artist: Frank E. Pape
Title: Tobacco Plantation in Nyasaland
Top Caption: Smoke Empire Tobacco
Displayed: June 1929
Printer: Johnson, Riddle and Co. Ltd., London
Size: 60 ins. × 40 ins.
EMB ref: AU5
PRO ref: CO 956/94

FRUIT   Locust Beans   **CYPRUS**   Asbestos   Silk

PLATE 42
Artist: Keith Henderson
Title: Cyprus
Top Caption: Some Empire Islands
Displayed: September 1929
Printer: John Horn Ltd., London and Glasgow
Size: 60 ins. × 40 ins.
EMB ref: AY3
PRO ref: CO 956/97

PLATE 43
Artist: F.C. Herrick
Title: Buy South African Oranges
Buy Canadian Hams and Bacon
Top Caption: Buy Empire Goods from Home and
Overseas
Displayed: September (?) 1929
Printer: Eyre and Spottiswoode Ltd., London
Size: 60 ins. × 40 ins.
EMB ref: AZ5
PRO ref: CO 956/114

JAFFA

PLATE 44
Artist: Frank Newbould
Title: Jaffa
Top Caption: Buy Jaffa Oranges
Displayed: December 1929
Printer: Waterlow and Sons Ltd., London,
Dunstable, Watford
Size: 60 ins. × 40 ins.
EMB ref: BA5
PRO ref: CO 956/125

DAIRYING IN AUSTRALIA

PLATE 45
Artist: Frank Newbould
Title: Dairying in Australia
Top Caption: Empire Buying Makes Busy
Factories
Displayed: April–May 1930
Printer: Waterlow and Sons Ltd., London,
Dunstable, Watford
Size: 60 ins. × 40 ins.
EMB ref: BM1
PRO ref: CO 956/175

STEEL MANUFACTURING IN THE UNITED KINGDOM

PLATE 46
Artist: Frank Newbould
Title: Steel Manufacturing in the United Kingdom
Top Caption: Empire Buying Makes Busy
Factories
Displayed: April-May 1930
Printer: Waterlow and Sons Ltd., London,
Dunstable, Watford
Size: 60 ins. × 40 ins.
EMB ref: BM5
PRO ref: CO 956/179

A SOUTH AFRICAN FRUIT FARM

B.O.I. ISSUED BY THE EMPIRE MARKETING BOARD.

PRINTED FOR H.M. STATIONERY OFFICE BY JOHN HORN LIMITED LONDON & GLASGOW

PLATE 47
Artist: Austin Cooper
Title: A South African Fruit Farm
Top Caption: Empire Buying Makes Busy
Factories
Displayed: August-September 1930
Printer: John Horn Ltd., London and Glasgow
Size: 60 ins. × 40 ins.
EMB ref: BO1
PRO ref: CO 956/187

EAST·AFRICAN TRANSPORT~OLD STYLE

PLATE 48
Artist: Adrian Allinson
Title: East African Transport - Old Style
Top Caption: Colonial Progress Brings Home
Prosperity
Displayed: December 1930-January 1931
Printer: Waterlow and Sons Ltd., London,
Dunstable, Watford
Size: 60 ins. × 40 ins.
EMB ref: BR1
PRO ref: CO 956/211

EAST·AFRICAN TRANSPORT — NEW STYLE

PLATE 49
Artist: Adrian Allinson
Title: East African Transport - New Style
Top Caption: Colonial Progress Brings Home
Prosperity
Displayed: December 1930-January 1931
Printer: Waterlow and Sons Ltd., London,
Dunstable, Watford
Size: 60 ins. × 40 ins.
EMB ref: BR5
PRO ref: CO 956/215

Cabot   Hudson   Drake   Smith   Raleigh   Dampier   Penn   Anson   Chatham   Wolfe   Clive

PLATE 50
Artist: Fred Taylor
Title: Cabot...Clive
Top Caption: The Empire is Still in Building
Displayed: September–October 1930
Printer: Waterlow and Sons Ltd., London,
Dunstable, Watford
Size: 60 ins. × 40 ins.
EMB ref: BT1
PRO ref: CO 956/223

PLATE 51
Artist: Frank Newbould
Title: Canadian Lumbermen
Top Caption: The Empire is Still in Building
Displayed: September–October 1930
Printer: Waterlow and Sons Ltd., London,
Dunstable, Watford
Size: 60 ins. × 40 ins.
EMB ref: BT3
PRO ref: CO 956/225

Cook Pitt Hastings Raffles Durham Sturt Brooke Lawrence Gordon Livingstone Rhodes

PLATE 52
Artist: Fred Taylor
Title: Cook...Rhodes
Top Caption: The Empire is Still in Building
Displayed: September-October 1930
Printer: Waterlow and Sons Ltd., London,
Dunstable, Watford
Size: 60 ins. × 40 ins.
EMB ref: BT5
PRO ref: CO 956/227

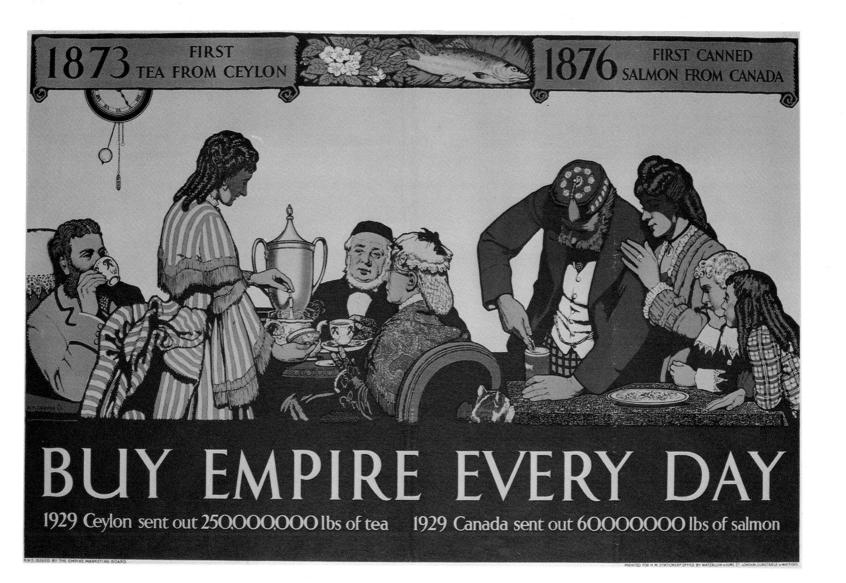

PLATE 53
Artist: R.T. Cooper
Title: Buy Empire Every Day
Top Caption: Milestones of Empire Trade
Displayed: January-February 1931
Printer: Waterlow and Sons Ltd., London,
Dunstable, Watford
Size: 60 ins. × 40 ins.
EMB ref: CO 956/245

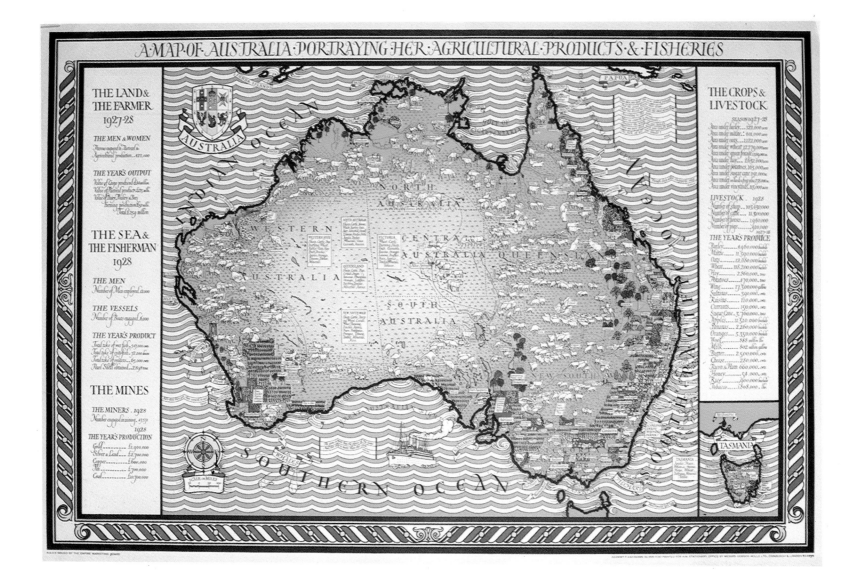

PLATE 54
Artist: MacDonald Gill
Title: A Map of Australia Portraying her
Agricultural Products and Fisheries
Top Caption: Let the Empire Flourish
Displayed: April-May 1931
Printer: Dobson Molle Ltd., Edinburgh and
London
Size: 60 ins. × 40 ins.
EMB ref: RBX5 (reprint for schools and public
purchase)
PRO ref: CO 956/521

THE MARKET GARDEN OF THE TROPICS — MALAYAN PINEAPPLES

PLATE 55
Artist: Edgar Ainsworth
Title: The Market Garden of the Tropics -
Malayan Pineapples
Top Caption: Buy from the Empire's Gardens
Displayed: May 1931
Printer: Johnson, Riddle and Co. Ltd., London
Size: 60 ins. × 40 ins.
EMB ref: CB1
PRO ref: CO 956/269

PLATE 56A
Artist: Edgar Ainsworth
Title: Borneo Sago
Top Caption: Buy from the Empire's Gardens
Displayed: May 1931
Printer: Johnson, Riddle and Co. Ltd., London
Size: 25 ins. × 40 ins.
EMB ref: CB2
PRO ref: CO 956/270

AND WE'LL ALL HAVE TEA

PLATE 56B
Artist: Keith Henderson
Title: And We'll All Have Tea
Top Caption: Empire Buying Makes Busy
Factories
Displayed: April-May 1930
Printer: Johnson, Riddle and Co. Ltd., London
Size: 25 ins. × 40 ins.
EMB ref: BN2
PRO ref: CO 956/182

NORTHERN IRELAND FLAX GROWING

PLATE 57
Artist: J. Humbert Craig
Title: Northern Ireland Flax Growing
Top Caption: The Home Countries First
Displayed: September–October (?) 1932
Printer: Waterlow and Sons Ltd., London,
Dunstable, Watford
Size: 60 ins. × 40 ins.
EMB ref: CE3
PRO ref: CO 956/287

MUTTON LAMB APPLES

PLATE 58
Artist: Frank Newbould
Title: Mutton Lamb Apples
Top Caption: Buy New Zealand Produce
Displayed: April (?) 1932
Printer: St. Michael's Press Ltd., West Norwood, London
Size: 60 ins. × 40 ins.
EMB ref: CH3
PRO ref: CO 956/304

THERE'S ALL THE HEALTH OF THE SEA IN FISH

PLATE 59
Artist: Charles Pears
Title: There's All the Health of the Sea in Fish
Top Caption: Caught by British Fishermen
Displayed: August–September 1931
Printer: Waterlow and Sons Ltd., London,
Dunstable, Watford
Size: 60 ins. × 40 ins.
EMB ref: CJ1
PRO ref: CO 956/308

PLATE 60
Artist: Charles Pears
Title: More than Half the Catch is Sold as Fried Fish
Top Caption: Caught by British Fishermen
Displayed: August-September 1931
Printer: Waterlow and Sons Ltd., London, Dunstable, Watford
Size: 60 ins. × 40 ins.
EMB ref: CJ3
PRO ref: CO 956/310

BACK COVER
Artist: Horace Taylor
Title: Follow the Empire Makers
Printer: John Horn Ltd., London and Glasgow
Size: 20 ins. × 30 ins.
EMB ref: SWB10
PRO ref: CO 956/553

Printed for Her Majesty's Stationery Office by William Clowes Ltd
Dd 738622 C75 9/86